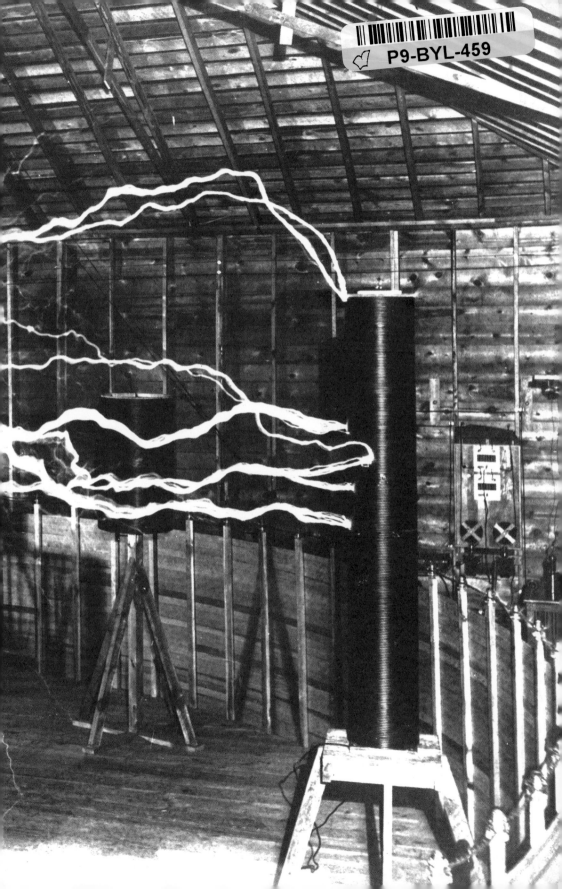

TESLA LABORATORY
LONG ISLAND N.Y.

New York Sept. 4 1895

Mr. F. G. Carpenter

My dear Sir,

Since the destruction of my
former laboratory I have learned
that I have great many friends
in your profession. I am afraid
we can not agree as to the article
but I can assure you that I
shall be pleased to make your
personal acquaintance. You will
find my at my laboratory 46 East
Houston Street any day from 10–12
A.M. and 3–7 P.M. If this time
should be inconvenient you may
call any time during the day,
it is probable you will find me.

Yours very truly

N. Tesla

Compliments from

Nikola Tesla

FALL RIVER PRESS

New York

An Imprint of Sterling Publishing
387 Park Avenue South
New York, NY 10016

FALL RIVER PRESS and the distinctive Fall River Press logo
are registered trademarks of Barnes & Noble, Inc.

Cover and book design by Scott Russo

ISBN 978-1-4351-4297-8

Distributed in Canada by Sterling Publishing
c/o Canadian Manda Group, 165 Dufferin Street
Toronto, Ontario, Canada M6K 3H6

Distributed in the United Kingdom by GMC Distribution Services
Castle Place, 166 High Street, Lewes, East Sussex, England BN7 1XU

Distributed in Australia by Capricorn Link (Australia) Pty. Ltd.
P.O. Box 704, Windsor, NSW 2756, Australia

For information about custom editions, special sales, and premium and corporate purchases,
please contact Sterling Special Sales at 800-805-5489 or specialsales@sterlingpublishing.com.

Manufactured in China

8 10 9 7

www.sterlingpublishing.com

Tesla

The Wizard of Electricity

by David J. Kent

FALL RIVER PRESS

New York

REC-33 100-2237-13

November 27, 1962

Dear ▓▓▓▓▓▓

Your letter of November 21st has been received.

In response to your inquiry, I would like to point
out that the effects of Dr. Nikola Tesla were impounded, after
his death, by the Office of Alien Property of the Department of
Justice and not by the FBI. Since this Bureau did not participate
in the handling of Dr. Tesla's effects, I am unable to supply the
information you desire.

Sincerely yours,

J. Edgar Hoover

John Edgar Hoover
Director

NOTE: Bufiles contain no record identifiable with correspondent.
Bufile 100-2237 shows that Dr. Tesla was one of the world's
outstanding scientists in the electrical field, and at the time of
his death, all of his personal papers and effects were believed
dangerous to the country's security if they fell into unauthorized
hands. The book, "Prodigal Genius," by John J. O'Neil, alleges
that the FBI took over a certain safe and opened it, appropriating
Dr. Tesla's property. Bufiles clearly indicate that it was the Office
of Alien Property of the Department which did so, and the above reply
has been forwarded in answer to related inquiries. Dr. Tesla was
born in Yugoslavia and died in New York City 1-7-43.

(3)

DEC 3 1962

MAIL ROOM ☐   TELETYPE UNIT ☐

For my parents Reginald and Florence
and
my son Bryan

All things are possible.

Contents

Opposite and throughout: "Prophet of Science,"
published in *Real Heroes*, no. 16, October 1946

Prologue

Like a rock star turning up the amp higher and higher to rock the house, Nikola Tesla turned up the vibrations on his tiny mechanical oscillator, which was connected to one of the iron support columns of his Houston Street laboratory. At first the vibrations seemed innocuous enough. Tesla's goal was merely to test his little oscillator. But his neighbors felt the shaking. Just a mild quivering in the beginning, no more than a heavy truck banging down the street in the distance. Then as the shaking persisted and grew stronger—and expanded further away from the laboratory—concern grew among the locals that they were experiencing a strong earthquake. In New York City? Startled residents in the nearby Italian and Chinese neighborhoods rushed into the streets in fear of being crushed by falling walls, cut by shattering glass, and shaken to pieces by the horrific trembling.

The local police on Mulberry Street felt it too. With a station around the corner from Tesla's laboratory they were all too familiar with the strange lights and sounds emanating from that particular building. But this was new. The ground was shaking, furniture was moving, pipes were breaking, and officers feared that the police headquarters itself was shaking apart. As windows started breaking from the harmonic vibrations, some of the policemen kept their wits enough to grasp the obvious conclusion—it was Tesla!

So off they went, rushing down the street and up into the building containing Tesla's laboratory. Overcoming their fear that the building would collapse around them, they surged through the door just as Tesla was swinging a heavy sledgehammer against the surprisingly small oscillator device, smashing it off the iron column and instantly stopping the vibrations.

Turning to see the unexpected presence of two uniformed police officers staring at him in shock, and still holding the sledgehammer in his hands, Tesla approached the two men in his usual calm and dignified manner. He explained himself:

"Gentlemen, I am sorry, but you are just a trifle too late to witness my experiment. I found it necessary to stop it suddenly and unexpectedly and in an unusual way just as you entered. If you will come around this evening I will have another oscillator attached to this platform and each of you can stand on it. You will, I am sure, find it a most interesting and pleasurable experience. Now you must leave, for I have many things to do. Good day, gentlemen."[1]

Tesla did not have a clue that he had nearly destroyed the neighborhood.

Nikola Tesla may be one of the most important men of invention in our nation's history, and yet many people have never heard of him. In a life that spanned more than eighty-six years, from just prior to the U.S. Civil War to the middle of World War II, the Serbo-Croatian born, but proudly naturalized American, was an eccentric genius who out-invented Edison and discovered radio before Marconi. Tesla's inventions include the alternating current system that powers our homes today, as well as radio, wireless transmission of energy and light, X-rays, and the electrifying Tesla coil. He also worked on development of direct energy weapons (death rays), contradicted Einstein's theory of relativity, and designed precursors to the modern vertical takeoff and landing (VTOL) aircraft.

During his lifetime Tesla moved from what is now Croatia to Budapest to Paris, then on to New York, and after a period of time in Colorado Springs, back to New York City where he maintained two laboratories. Along the way he worked for Thomas Edison, but then became his biggest rival. He forged friendships with such divergent personalities as George Westinghouse, Mark Twain, Robert Underwood Johnson, John Muir, and a white pigeon. His many idiosyncrasies included an obsession with numbers divisible by three, ardent gambling, and a near-pathological fear of germs. While it was not uncommon for women to fall in love with him, Tesla intentionally remained celibate as a means of self-control, believing that it helped focus his scientific thinking. He rarely slept more than a few hours at a time, often going days without rest. While generally soft-spoken, he could be a consummate showman, sprinkling his lectures with seemingly magical displays of light and energy. His Tesla coil could send lightning surging through his body . . . or up to 135 feet into the air. He was a world-renowned scientist and socialite, yet in the end he died alone and nearly penniless, having ceded many millions of dollars in royalties to his friend George Westinghouse.

Tesla: The Wizard of Electricity takes us through Tesla's erratic yet exceptionally productive life, his innovative experiments and ground-breaking contributions to science, and brings us into his uniquely complex mind. While noting his many technical achievements, the book is written for the general reader so that everyone can appreciate and gain insights into the man himself. Those seeking some awareness of his many inventions will find the book enlightening. Those seeking to explore Tesla's personality, his trials and tribulations, and his impact on others will find the book eminently appealing.

Much of what we know about his life comes through his own writings, which include both prolific technical material and significant personal memories from his childhood. Therefore, this book draws from Tesla's own hand and the writings of others who knew him and his accomplishments. We explore Tesla's upbringing, his methods and discoveries, his many personality quirks, and some of the conspiracy theories that have grown around him. Finally, the book looks at his amazing—and lasting—legacy for the modern world, both in terms of the scientific advances still being made from his discoveries and how Tesla's mysterious aura has inspired a new generation of followers.

Opposite: Tesla peeking out of his lab in Colorado Springs, ca. 1895

A SCIENTIFIC ROCK STAR IS BORN

As though it had been ordered up by a filmmaker's special effects department, the threatening storm arrived just as Djouka Tesla went into labor. As she prayed for an easy delivery of her fourth child, the roar of the thunder drowned out her stifled cries. Precisely at midnight[1] the cries transferred from Djouka's lips to those of the newly born Nikola. In an omen that could not have been scripted more prophetically, a lightning bolt crackled from the sky and lit up the small house just as Nikola entered this world.

Startled, the midwife turned to the young mother and said "Your new son is a child of the storm."

"No," responded Djouka, "He is a child of the light."[2]

And so it seems that, from the beginning, Nikola Tesla was destined to electrify the world.

That warm July night in 1856 took place in Smiljan, a small village located in what was then the Austrian Empire but now is part of Croatia. Being born exactly at midnight led to some uncertainty as to the date his birthday should be celebrated, but in practice Tesla's birthdays were rarely celebrated much at all, at least until his later years when he was world famous. Then his birthdays (officially July 10) became celebrated affairs complete with press coverage. But that was much later. For now he was just the son of a Serbian Orthodox priest in a tiny country hamlet.

Family

In Smiljan, Nikola's father, Milutin Tesla, was the local pastor, one of the few career choices for an educated Serbian-born man living in the Austrian Territories. The son of a military officer, Milutin initially followed the path of his father's footsteps. He soon found out, however, that the rigidity of military life was not for him and, finding an excuse in criticism over improperly burnished buttons, Milutin abruptly departed military school.

Always a literate man, Milutin spent his days writing poetry and political discourse, the latter of which he signed with a pseudonym, Srbin Pravicich, meaning "Man of Justice" in his native Serb.[3]

Above: Tesla's birth certificate
Right: Tesla's father Milutin and mother Djouka

Eventually Milutin met Djouka Mandić, the daughter of a prominent Serbian family, and he soon found himself in love. No doubt influenced by the many priests in Djouka's family tree, Milutin developed a desire to study for the clergy. He quickly completed his studies, was ordained an Orthodox priest, and placed as pastor of a small church in the important seaport of Senj along the Croatian coast.[4] Several years and three children later, Milutin impressed the new archbishop with his unusual, if not awe-inspiring, sermon on the fruits of labor. This "best sermon performance" in the diocese earned him a privileged red sash and, not long after, a promotion to lead the larger parish at Smiljan. It was here that Nikola and his younger sister Marica were born.

From his father Nikola learned the literate life. In addition to his skills with poetry and his philosophical articles, Milutin was a master

Above: Tesla's house in Smiljan, Croatia

of several languages, being able to converse as well as read and write in Serbo-Croat, German, and Italian. No doubt because of this influence Nikola himself became a polyglot, eventually outdoing his father by being able to speak and read at least eight different languages.[5] In contrast, Nikola's mother was unable to read or write. Though her family was very well educated—her father was a Serbian Orthodox priest like her future husband was to become—Djouka was forced to take over the role of homemaker when her mother's eyesight, always tentative, failed completely while Djouka was still very young.[6]

Perhaps this sudden head-of-household status forced her to become more inventive and warranting of Tesla's later description of his mother as "a truly great woman, of rare skill, courage and fortitude."[7] He also credited her with instilling his own legendary work ethic and stamina. While Tesla's linguistic and literary talents were driven by his father, there is no doubt that his mother was his inventive inspiration. Originally from western Serbia, Djouka Mandić was from one of the oldest families in the country. Their heritage was one of stout stock, or as Tesla put it in 1917, he came from a "wiry and long-lived race."[8] He boasted that some of his ancestors had been centenarians, living in excess of one hundred years. In fact, Tesla boldly, if perhaps implausibly, asserted "one of them lived one hundred and twenty-nine years." In any case, since Tesla lived to be eighty-six years old himself, we can presume that he came from very good stock indeed.

Tesla referred to his ancestors on his mother's side as "a line of inventors." According to Tesla, Djouka's father and grandfather had designed "numerous implements for household, agricultural and other uses," and Djouka followed suit with her own inventions.[9]

Tesla practically gushed at her accomplishments in his 1919 autobiography, *My Inventions*. He declared that:

"my mother was an inventor of the first order and had she not had the misfortune of living in a region so remote from modern life would have achieved great things."[10]

Opposite: Tesla, aged 23, ca. 1879

Like Tesla himself throughout his career, his mother worked tirelessly from "the break of day till late at night," inventing and constructing all kinds of tools and devices. She also was a talented weaver and seamstress, even to the point of planting and harvesting the vegetation she used to make by hand most of the apparel and home furnishings used by the large family. Tesla marveled at her continued dexterity long into her old age, noting that "when she was past sixty, her fingers were still nimble enough to tie three knots in an eyelash." Presumably the eyelash was no longer implanted above the eye at the time.

As the fourth child and second son, Nikola was relegated to the background during his early years; tradition focused its resources on the eldest son, Dane. By all accounts Dane exhibited extraordinary talent and potential. He was loved dearly by Milutin and Djouka, as he was by Nikola and his sisters Milka, Angelina, and baby girl Marica. But this situation was to change abruptly when Nikola became the only male heir after Dane's rather mysterious death. As Tesla later tells it,[11] Dane met his end at the hands, or rather the hooves, of the family horse. The horse itself had previously been a favorite of the Tesla family as it had supposedly "saved my father's life under remarkable circumstances." Referring to the horse as a "magnificent" Arabian breed, Tesla relates the story:

"My father had been called one winter night to perform an urgent duty and while crossing the mountains, infested by wolves, the horse became frightened and ran away, throwing him violently to the ground. It arrived home bleeding and exhausted, but after the alarm was sounded immediately dashed off again, returning to the spot, and before the searching party were far on the way they were met by my father, who had recovered consciousness and remounted, not realizing he had been lying in the snow for several hours."[12]

So his father was saved by the rather temperamental horse. Twelve-year-old brother Dane was not so lucky. Again according to Tesla, "this horse was responsible for my brother's injuries from which he died." Worse yet, five-year-old Nikola "witnessed the tragic scene" and the "visual impression of it has lost none of its force" over the half-century that had elapsed between its occurrence and Tesla's written memoirs.[13]

Others suggest that Nikola may not have been such an innocent bystander, but we will never know. Nikola never expanded upon his role in this tragic event nor provided any substantive details. His parents were devastated and too distraught to ever discuss it. Whatever happened, at a very tender age Nikola was now the eldest son. Neither he nor his parents ever fully recovered emotionally from Dane's untimely demise. What did happen was that his parents transferred their high expectations for Dane to the much younger Nikola, and Nikola himself assumed the burdens of both replacing his older brother and seeking his own greatness. This strain may be part of the reason why Nikola developed some rather interesting oddities.

Tesla barely mentions his three sisters in his writings. We do know that he sent money home to his mother and sisters once he was established in New York City.[14] And that they had done what many daughters of clergymen did in those days—married good priests and bore children. Tesla did exchange correspondence with them, or more accurately, mostly with their husbands, since he once admitted to an uncle that "somehow it is hard to correspond with the ladies."[15] Occasionally he would write his sisters directly, usually to send checks because, after all, Nikola was the "star of the family"[16] and likely loved them dearly.[17]

In contrast to the obvious love and admiration for his immediate family, Tesla's memories of other relatives are not always so flattering. A good example is the story he tells of his two aunts, a story that in retrospect is distinctly irreverent.[18] Apparently these two aunts were, well, not exactly the local beauty queens. They were old, at least in young Nikola's eyes, and quite wrinkled in their faces. One of them

Above: An old Serbian five-dinar coin

had "two teeth protruding like the tusks of an elephant." That vision must have been ghastly enough to a child, but she had a habit of burying these tusks in Tesla's cheek every time she kissed him. In traditional Serbian culture this happens quite a lot, and most certainly too often for Tesla's liking. Being quite affectionate and adoring of their young nephew, the aunts kissed and hugged him to their heart's content. To Tesla, this was a fate worse than death. "Nothing could scare me more," said Tesla, "than the prospect of being hugged by these as affectionate as unattractive relatives."[19]

One day an incident occurred that likely brought Tesla's family more than a modicum of embarrassment. Djouka was carrying Nikola in her arms, and perhaps not anticipating the lack of political correctness of the young lad, unfortunately decided to ask Nikola which of the two aunts he thought was prettier. Already the diligent observer that would later become the famous inventor, Tesla studied the faces of the two aunts intently. After careful thought he pointed to one of them and proudly declared,

"This here is not as ugly as the other."

While we do not know their reactions, we can assume young Nikola was not so warmly hugged after that.

Youthful Excitement

Tesla was far from being merely the nerdy kid who did not experience the normal life of a child. Having grown up in rural Croatia, when not doing chores around the house Tesla, like most children, managed to get into more than a few scrapes. He admits that he was a constant concern to his parents who, especially after the frequently evoked memory of his older brother's death, knew Nikola was their only chance to carry on the family name. Ah, but young Nikola's "youth and lightheartedness" brought him into "innumberable [*sic*] difficulties, dangers and scrapes" from which he "extricated himself as if by enchantment."[20]

Once he fell into a tank of hot milk.[21] On another occasion he was attacked by the family goose.[22] Then there was the time he tried to fly with the aid of nothing more than a frail old umbrella. That particular bit of fanciful thinking put him in bed recuperating for the next six weeks.[23]

Tesla loved to tell of these youthful exploits. Even on such a momentous occasion as accepting the Edison Medal from the prestigious American Institute of Electrical Engineers (AIEE, now the Institute of Electrical and Electronics Engineers, IEEE) Tesla recounted some of his youthful trials and tribulations:

"I was almost cremated three or four times and just missed being boiled alive. I was buried, abandoned and frozen. I have had narrow escapes from mad dogs, hogs, and other wild animals. I have passed through dreadful diseases—have been given up by physicians three or four times in my life for good. I have met with all sorts of odd accidents—I cannot think of anything that did not happen to me, and to realize that I am here this evening, hale and hearty, young in mind and body, with all these fruitful years behind me, is little short of a miracle."[24]

Tesla was certainly not a man for understatement.

First Efforts at Invention

With inspiration from his mother and necessity from being a child of the country, Tesla showed his inventive streak at a very young age. Like most children of the time, Tesla often wandered off to the old fishing hole to engage in sport and hunt for that evening's dinner. One day a local boy had managed to acquire a hook and fishing tackle as a gift from a visiting relative. Off the boy went, with his gear in hand and a veritable posse of neighborhood buddies following him, to the local pond to try to catch frogs. Tesla was not so lucky—he had quarreled with the boy and was left deserted as they marched off laughing.[25]

Feeling eager to show the others he could do it too, but with the disadvantage of never having seen a real fish hook in his life, Tesla created his first invention. He imagined that a real hook was "something wonderful, endowed with peculiar qualities" that somehow lured frogs like a siren lures sailors to their deaths upon the rocky shores. But even at the tender age of five Nikola was resourceful and set his mind to work.

Soon after the family moved to Gospić Tesla had a chance to show his quick thinking and inventiveness. A new man-powered fire pump apparatus had been purchased to replace the ineffective bucket brigade. The day of testing was filled with excitement until the order for the sixteen hefty men to start pumping was given, and nothing happened—"not a drop of water came out of the nozzle."[27] Despite having no idea how the apparatus worked, the seven-year-old Tesla quickly realized there must be a kink in the hose used to draw water from the river. Off went his clothes and into the river he jumped. A quick twisting of the hose and all was well—the water sprayed high into the air, and then down onto the unsuspecting crowd of officials and townspeople. The fire team had been so distracted by Tesla's antics that they forgot where they had the nozzle pointed.

Finding some soft iron wire, he grabbed two small stones and hammered the end of the wire until it formed a sharp point. With a little bend to get it into a hook shape, some strong string, and a pole made from a conveniently located branch, Nikola had his own homemade fishing gear and invented an innovative method to capture the frogs. Before long, all the boys in the village were armed with this "infallible" technique, and they "brought disaster to the frogs."[26]

But jigging frogs was merely a prelude to his exploits with May bugs (what we call June bugs)—exploits that led to his first true efforts to "harness the energies of nature in the service of man," efforts that would dominate Tesla's life for much of his eight decades. When Tesla was five he had invented a sort of waterwheel consisting of a simple smooth disk made of wood, a prelude to the bladeless turbine he would invent in later life.[28] And when he was nine years old he came up with an idea that was pure genius. Tesla put together two strips of wood in a windmill shape and glued them to a spindle, just like a more modern child's toy. But Tesla went further by attaching a small set of pulleys and thread to create an engine of sorts. For a power source he captured quite a number of May bugs, sixteen of which he glued to the four blades of the windmill. As the May bugs tried to escape, their frantically beating wings acted in consort to spin the windmill at relatively high speed, which then turned the larger pulley system at lower speed but with a "surprisingly large torque."[29]

Unfortunately, a neighborhood boy later gobbled down the cache of May bugs, an act that so repulsed Tesla that he instantly gave up his plan to build a "one-hundred-bug-power" motor.[30] We'll never know how far Tesla could have taken this idea.

Life Takes a New Turn

One of the most important events of his youth, however, came with regards to Tesla's childhood cat Mačak. As Tesla relates in a letter to a friend's daughter, at one point during a cold snowy day Tesla "felt impelled to stroke Mačak's back."[31] He notes that what he saw "was a miracle which made me speechless . . . Mačak's back was a sheet of light, and my hand produced a shower of crackling sparks loud enough to be heard all over the place." Tesla's father explained that this must be caused by electricity, like that of lightning, and this thought convinced Tesla that he wanted to pursue becoming an "electrician."

This experience with Mačak kept Tesla wondering how to harness the amazing electrical power of nature. But first Tesla had to overcome the tradition that required him to enter a course of study for the clergy. After all, his father was a clergyman and with Dane gone the duty of following in his father's footsteps fell to Nikola. Doing so was also "the fondest wishes" of the mother he so adored.[32] But to Tesla the idea was abhorrent. "This prospect hung like a dark cloud on my mind," he later wrote in his personal recollections.[33] It simply had no appeal to him. His mind was just too inquisitive, too demanding of deep thought, too eager to explore the development of new ideas. No, the clergy was definitely not something to which Tesla aspired.

Then he got sick. And his life, while at first in danger of being extinguished, took a whole new turn.

Cholera was a deadly disease in the 1800s, especially in villages like those where Tesla grew up. An epidemic of cholera took off in Tesla's native land and nothing could be done to battle it. "People knew nothing of the character of the disease," Tesla would later relate, and sanitation was nearly nonexistent. Tesla lamented the lack of understanding of the causes of the epidemic. The townspeople "burned huge piles of odorous shrubbery to purify the air," thinking that somehow the stench would stem the horrible tide of death. Or perhaps it was merely to cover up the stench of death itself. In any case, the real problem was the water, and the people "drank freely of the infected water and died in crowds like sheep."[34]

Tesla at the time was away from home, just finishing his eleven years of public education. Unfortunately, rather than staying away—and against "peremptory [sic] orders" from his father—Tesla rushed home to Gospić. Stricken down with cholera almost immediately upon his return, Tesla spent the next nine months struggling to stay alive with "scarcely the ability to move" and exhausted of all vitality. Despite being given up for

Opposite: A typically fantastical representation of Tesla in his lab

dead by the local physicians, who must have been right most of the time given the number of people who succumbed, Tesla survived the experience "on account of my intense desire to live." His father still wanted Nikola to join the clergy, but in an effort to stimulate the life forces of his ailing son, promised to let Tesla study engineering should he recover.[35]

After hearing this, Tesla's recovery was miraculous. His desire to live restored, Tesla showed amazing vitality in less than a week, something quite unexpected after nearly nine months of constant illness. Perhaps as a result of having the onus of the priesthood lifted off his shoulders (or perhaps as a result of creative memory from a resourceful man decades later), Tesla returned to health quickly with the knowledge that he was to enter engineering school within only a few months.[36]

His childhood was over. And his long and eventful path toward becoming (as some termed him) "the inventor of the 20th Century" was about to begin.[37]

Below: The first photograph ever taken by phosphorescent light, 1894. The face is Tesla's, and the light source is one of his phosphorescent bulbs

TESLA LABORATORY
LONG ISLAND N.Y.

(No Model.)

N. TESLA.
MEANS FOR GENERATING ELECTRIC CURRENTS.

No. 514,168.   Patented Feb. 6, 1894.

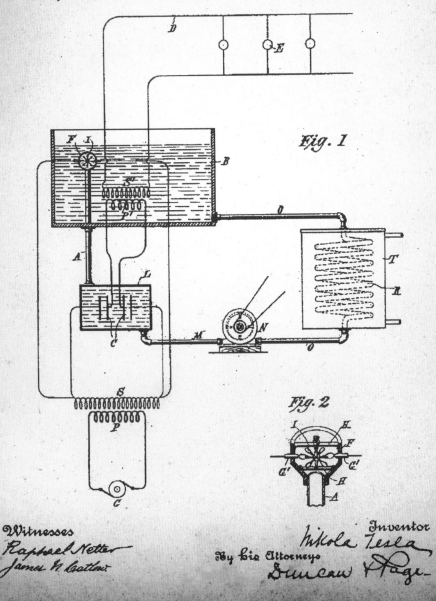

Fig. 1

Fig. 2

Witnesses
Raphael Netter
James H. Catline

Inventor
Nikola Tesla
By his Attorneys
Duncan & Page

COMING OF AGE IN EUROPE

By the second half of the 1800s the city of Graz, near what is now the southern border of Austria with Slovenia, was already an important center of education. What would become the Graz University of Technology was founded by the Archduke John of Austria in 1811 for the purpose of teaching physics, chemistry, astronomy, mineralogy, botany, and technology. By 1875 when the nineteen-year-old Tesla arrived at the school—then named the Technische Hochschule (Institute of Technology)—it had been taken over by the state and had already grown into one of the premier engineering schools in the region. Some of the best and the brightest students learned from some of the best and the brightest professors.[1] This is exactly where Tesla wanted to be.

But first there was the question of money. His father's income as an Orthodox priest was not enough to send Tesla to a top-of-the-line university, so they sought the money from the military instead. But it came with a catch—Tesla would have to join the army for eight years after he graduated. Later this would lead to a rather mysterious year hiding in the mountains, for health reasons, which ultimately voided his commitment to military service. Dubious as this adventure sounds, the arrangement did allow Tesla to enter the prestigious technical school.

By all accounts Tesla was a hard-working student.[2] In his first year he took eleven courses. He passed his course examinations for nine of them, doubling the usual output required for students. Besides arithmetic, geometry, theoretical and applied physics, machinery construction, wave theory, and optics—courses you would expect in an engineering school—Tesla also took mineralogy, botany, French, and English.[3] To this he later added other languages—a polyglot, he eventually could speak about eight languages—and studied the works of great thinkers such as Goethe, Descartes, and Shakespeare.

The dean of the technical faculty was so impressed that he wrote Tesla's father:

"Your son is a star of the first rank."[4]

Rather than being the proud father, Milutin Tesla was aghast at the near mania he saw in his son's study habits. The mere four hours of "rest" each night was taking a toll on Nikola's health. So like in Nikola's early years when his father would scold him for reading in the candlelight to the wee hours of the morning, Milutin criticized Nikola for his poor physical and mental condition.[5] Perplexed at the apparent lack of parental pride in his accomplishments, Tesla would only years later discover that the professor had asked Milutin to remove Nikola from school "as he was in danger of killing himself from overwork."[6]

Tesla's schedule in his second year at Graz was less manic. Completing only the normal workload of five courses,[7] he focused on physics, mechanics, and mathematics.[8] Tesla planned on becoming a professor and so took classes with such eminent instructors as Professor Rogner (known for his "histrionics"); Professor Poeschl (known for being "punctilious"), and Professor Allé.[9] Tesla especially liked Professor

Allé, with whom he studied integral calculus.[10] Allé was the most brilliant lecturer to whom I ever listened, said Tesla in his autobiography.[11] Allé had taken special interest and would stay after hours, according to Tesla, giving me problems to solve, in which I delighted.[12]

The Commutator Question

Electricity was still in its infancy when Tesla attended the university. Most electricity generation at the time relied on a direct current system. Just four years before Tesla entered Graz, Zénobe Gramme had demonstrated his new machine, the first generator to produce power on a commercial scale for industry, to the Academy of Sciences in Paris.[13] Now in his second year of studies, Tesla was able to see a Gramme machine firsthand.[14]

Professor Poeschl's classroom that day was buzzing with excitement. While the university was known for having the best resources, Gramme machines were still a rarity. Poeschl had obtained one and would demonstrate its use. The machine could act as either a source of power or a motor. This latter fact was actually a new revelation. Gramme had only recently discovered that his machine, if supplied with constant voltage, could act as an electric motor. In a bit of serendipity, his partner had carelessly connected the terminals of a Gramme machine

Above: The Gramme machine

to another dynamo that was producing electricity, and suddenly the shaft began to turn. Today this design is still the basis for nearly all direct current electric motors.[15]

As Poeschl demonstrated the Gramme machine Tesla immediately observed its major flaw. As the wire-wrapped soft iron ring that made up the rotor turned, it required a commutator—a simple rotary electrical switch, required by all direct current systems, that applies power to the best location of the rotor as it turns—to reverse the current direction, a necessity since the normal turning of the rotor naturally changes the current in the winding with each half turn.[16]

But the sparks! The commutator sparked like a mini-fireworks display. Tesla, never one to be inhibited when he felt he was right, offered to Poeschl that this was a major defect in the design. Not surprisingly, Poeschl somewhat indignantly replied that "it is inherent in the nature of the machine."[17] Further, he explained, "as long as electricity flows in one direction, and as long as [a] magnet has two poles each of which acts oppositely on the current, we will have to use a commutator to change, at the right moment, the direction of the current in the rotating armature."

Tesla refused to back down. He retorted, "That is obvious. The machine is limited by the current used. I am suggesting that we get rid of the commutator entirely by using alternating current."[18]

Being challenged by the twenty-year-old country boy apparently did not sit well with the experienced Professor Poeschl, who decided to use his next lecture to methodically, and brutally, tear apart Tesla's idea. Even Tesla himself was dumbfounded by the thoroughness and the public nature of the rebuke. Poeschl finished his embarrassment of Tesla with:

"Mr. Tesla will accomplish great things, but he certainly will never do this. It would be equivalent to converting a steady pulling force like gravity into rotary effort. It is a perpetual motion scheme, an impossible idea."

At that moment, Nikola Tesla dedicated his every thought to proving that Poeschl was wrong and that he, Tesla, was right. The idea became an obsession. For the rest of his second year at Graz, and into his third, he struggled to visualize an electrical machine that would work without the dreaded commutator. His lack of success was frustrating but he knew that he would eventually discover the way. That discovery would take several more years to bring to fruition.

But not at Graz. For reasons still unclear even today, Tesla never finished his studies at Graz. He went from a superman taking eleven classes in his first year, to a mere five the second, and then never completed any tests beyond the first semester of his third year. Sure, he had picked up some bad habits like gambling, cards, and billiards, but his mind was still as sharp as ever. Needless to say, Tesla's father—who had once worried that Nikola would work himself to death—was not particularly happy to see his son return home with the money Milutin had forwarded for the purpose of going to Prague to finish his studies. Indeed, rather than starting in the fall term in Prague, Tesla "lost himself," disappearing without a word. Eventually he went to Marburg (now called Maribor) in present-day Slovenia to take a job as an assistant engineer.

Finding Himself

Tesla had a difficult time in Marburg. While he received a very good salary, he also became a bit of a carouser.[19] He often went out with friends to drink and played cards on the streets with the locals.[20] After getting himself into trouble one too many times, he was forced by the local authorities to leave the city. Worried by his disappearance, Milutin was finally able to find his son and convinced him to return to Gospić. With financial help from his often-exasperated father, in 1880 Nikola headed to Prague with the goal of continuing his engineering studies at the prestigious Charles-Ferdinand University.

Prague in the late nineteenth century was an important city in the Habsburg era, and like Lika, the region that included Smiljan, it was part of the Austro-Hungarian empire. The previous German-speaking

majority had been replaced by an influx of Czech immigrants, but Tesla could speak both languages fluently so was never at a loss for words. Tesla arrived in time for the summer term and diligently threw himself into studying physics and mathematics as he pursued his dream of becoming an electrical engineer. He also continued to think hard about a motor without a commutator. He knew he would find the answer.

Then his father died.

No longer able to fund his education, Tesla left the university in Prague, never again to return to formal education and never to earn an academic degree. He was off to get a job. Luckily, at least so he thought, a family contact could get him a job in Budapest at the new telephone central station. Tesla hopped on a train and headed for the Hungarian capital ready to work on Alexander Graham Bell's new telephone.

Unfortunately for Tesla, the telephone exchange had not yet been built. In fact, it had not yet even been designed. Frustrated by the mis-communication but in need of basic food, clothing, and shelter, Tesla took a job working in the Hungarian Central Telegraph Office as a draftsman.[21] The irony of drawing for his rather meager pay was not lost on Tesla, who had nearly failed out of his early schooling due to his inability to draw. Luckily his diligence, talent, and work ethic quickly propelled him into an engineering job where he could use his meticulousness and legendary vision to design the new telephone systems.[22]

Here Tesla finally felt like he was doing something worthwhile. Always willing and able to improve on existing designs, Tesla soon invented a new device to amplify sound—an early version of a loud speaker.[23] His first real invention also demonstrated what would later become more obvious, that is, Tesla was better at invention than at commercialization—he never patented the device. This was a trait that would create problem after problem for Tesla throughout his life.

Tesla worked closely with a family friend, Ferenc Puskas, who with his brother Tivadar had run Thomas Edison's lighting operations in St. Petersburg and the direct current exhibit at the Paris Exposition.[24] Here in Budapest Tesla learned from Puskas about Edison's already voluminous and momentous achievements. He also studied the principle

Previous: Ring Street, Budapest

of induction, and in his spare time, worked on the problem of getting rid of the commutator and inventing the alternating current induction motor. It was an obsession that Tesla later explained:

> "With me it was a sacred vow, a question of life or death. I knew that I would perish if I failed."[25]

And he almost did perish. His words were not mere hyperbole—his obsession with this problem did become a matter of life and death. His tendency toward obsessively long workdays and little sleep finally took its toll and Tesla had a nervous breakdown. Always afflicted with strange flashes of light and disturbed by excessive sounds, now even the slightest whisper could be unbearable. He claims that a ticking watch "three rooms away sounded like the beat of hammers on an anvil."[26] The smallest vibrations pounded through his body. A beam of sunlight felt like a laser on his skin. His heart beat up to 150 beats a minute. In short, Tesla was a mess.

The Discovery

For months Tesla fought his own demons, both physiological and psychological. Convulsions periodically wracked his body and mental fatigue drained him of the will to live. On top of his ailments, Tesla was also besieged with his continued failure to solve the problem of the commutator-less alternating current motor that had first become his obsession in Poeschl's lecture hall back in Graz. Likely the pursuit of this solution was what kept him going.

Part of his therapy, if you will, was to take daily walks, something that his friend Anton Szigeti had insisted upon. It was during one of these walks that Tesla made the discovery that would change his life and eventually put the world on the path to modern electricity.

Following: Tesla lecturing before the French Physical Society and The International Society of Electricians, ca. 1880

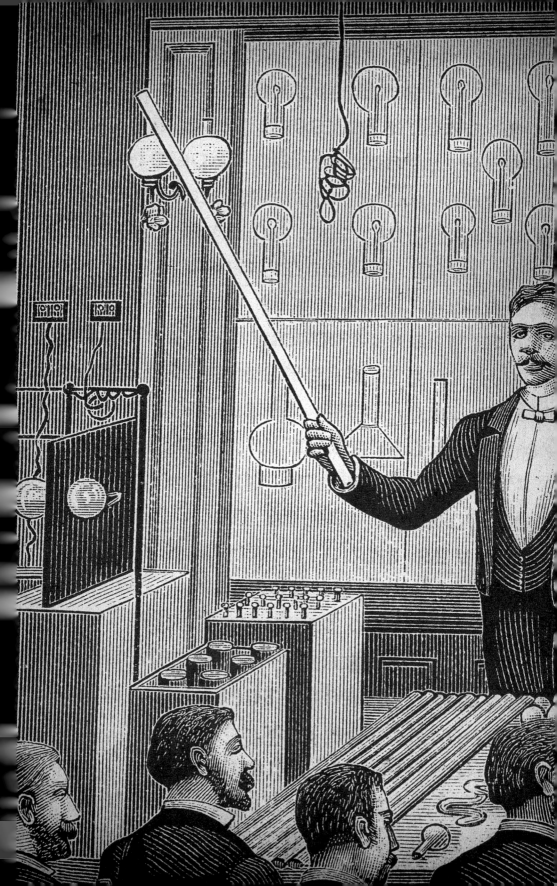

In 1882, Budapest was less than a decade past the official merging of the twin capital cities of Buda and Pest. Construction of the now imposing parliament building that dominates the Pest side of the Danube River would not be started for another three years, while high on the hill of the opposite bank the centuries-old Buda Castle was undergoing yet another remodeling as the city grew to accommodate its new role in the autonomous Hungarian government. Electric lighting—by direct current—had been installed in the city center in 1878.[27]

It was here that Tesla walked one evening with Szigeti as the sun slowly settled down over the horizon. The glistening sunset reminded Tesla of one of the many poems that he had memorized—from the tragic play *Faust* by Johann Wolfgang von Goethe.

As Tesla strolled in a near trance he recited aloud Goethe's famous lines in its original German:

Above: A view of Budapest, ca.1890–1900
Left: Poster for Dutch production of *Faust*, ca. 1918

"Sieruckt und weicht, der Tag istuberlebt, Dort eiltsiehin und fordertneuesLeben. Oh, dasskein Flugelmichvom Bodenhebt Ihrnach und immernachzustreben! EinschonerTraumindessensieentweicht, Ach, zu des Geistes Flugelnwird so leicht Keinkorperlicher Flugelsichgesellen!"

[The glow retreats, done is the day of toil; It yonder hastes, new fields of life exploring; Ah, that no wing can lift me from the soil Upon its track to follow, follow soaring! A glorious dream! though now the glories fade. Alas! the wings that lift the mind no aid Of wings to lift the body can bequeath me.][28]

Gasping, Tesla stopped suddenly. As he relates in his autobiography:

"As I uttered these inspiring words the idea came like a flash of lightning and in an instant the truth was revealed. I drew with a stick on the sand the diagrams… The images I saw were wonderfully sharp and clear and had the solidity of metal and stone, so much so that I told him: 'See my motor here; watch me reverse it.' I cannot begin to describe my emotions. Pygmalion seeing his statue come to life could not have been more deeply moved. A thousand secrets of nature which I might have stumbled upon accidentally I would have given for that one which I had wrested from her against all odds and at the peril of my existence."[29]

"The conception of a rotating magnetic field was a majestically beautiful one," his first biographer John O'Neill wrote fawningly, "it introduced to the scientific world a new principle of sublime grandeur whose simplicity and utility opened a vast new empire of useful applications." Tesla achieved what Professor Poeschl had said was impossible.[30]

The long-sought alternating current motor was invented, if only in his magnificently detailed imagination. It would be another six years before Tesla, by then working in New York City, would be cajoled by Thomas Commerford Martin into presenting the design in an address to the AIEE. For now the invention that would change the world remained in Tesla's head, in such intense detail that for the next several years he modified and improved on the device entirely through visualization. As Tesla later describes in *My Inventions*:

"For a while I gave myself up entirely to the intense enjoyment of picturing machines and devising new forms. It was a mental state of happiness about as complete as I have ever known in life. Ideas came in an uninterrupted stream and the only difficulty I had was to hold them fast.

The pieces of apparatus I conceived were to me absolutely real and tangible in every detail, even to the minute marks and signs of wear. I delighted in imagining the motors constantly running, for in this way they presented to mind's eye a more fascinating sight. When natural inclination develops into a passionate desire, one advances towards his goal in seven-league boots. In less than two months I evolved virtually all the types of motors and modifications of the system which are now identified with my name."[31]

An impressive claim, to be sure. Still, it would be years later before his new invention would actually be put into use.

Opposite: Thomas Edison (seated, center), ca. 1892

On to Paris

In 1882 Tesla's time in the Hungarian capital was coming to an end. His close relationship with the Puskas brothers led him to Charles Batchelor, who was Thomas Edison's man in Paris.[32] Batchelor was an Englishman and mechanic supreme, having learned his trade in the textile mills of Manchester.[33] But Batchelor was more than just a good technician; he was a natural salesman and organizer. Nearly single-handedly he had overseen the spread of Edison's direct current system across Europe, mostly as isolated power plants for individual factories, hotels, shipyards, and railroad stations.[34] This highlighted the big problem with direct current—it was limited to low voltages and could not be transmitted more than a short distance. Direct current power plants had to be installed every mile or so to light up a city, a logistical problem that meant despite his sales skills Batchelor was only able to install three central power stations, one each in the cities of Milan, Rotterdam, and St. Petersburg.

Tesla knew he had the answer to this problem—the alternating current induction motor. But newly arrived in Paris and taking a job as a junior engineer at Société Industrielle, part of the Compagnie Continental Edison, Tesla was hardly yet in a position to change the world. While he pitched his alternating current system to Batchelor and others in Paris, Edison's people simply did not want to listen. After all, theirs was the direct current system and Edison had invested himself completely in making and selling direct current throughout Europe, the United States, and the world. No, Edison thought, Tesla's alternating current system simply would not do.

As he had many times in the past, Tesla threw himself into work. Rising around five o'clock every morning, he kept a regular schedule of swimming twenty-seven laps at a bathhouse on the Seine river that snaked through Paris, then briskly walked an hour to the Edison factory, wolfed down a hearty "woodchopper's" breakfast, and then began a day that would generally take him to the wee hours of the next morning.[35]

Tesla worked hard, but he also played hard. He discovered that Paris was a magnet for high fashion and the arts. He developed a passion for fine clothes, often buying the most fashionable tailored suits, complete with soft kid leather gloves, high-end leather shoes with spats, and the finest handmade shirts. This penchant for finery and luxury was not, unfortunately, matched by his junior engineer salary, which meant "the income was spent as soon as received." When asked by Puskas how he was getting along in the new city Tesla described his situation and quipped humorously about his finances:

"The last twenty-nine days of the month are the toughest!"[36]

Tesla's time at Continental Edison was initially spent as a kind of traveling repairman sent to fix some of the tougher problems with the direct current system. Moving about mainly in France and Germany, he would "cure the ills" and return to Paris. This experience led him to propose improvements to the dynamos, which he implemented. "My success was complete," Tesla would write, "and the delighted directors accorded me the privilege of developing automatic regulators which were much desired." Having quickly built a reputation as someone who could save the day, not to mention his proficiency in the German language, Tesla was the obvious choice to send to Strasbourg, Alsace (part of Germany at the time, now Strasbourg, France). A catastrophic event had occurred during the opening ceremony of the new lighting plant at the railroad station, and help was needed fast.

The Strasbourg rail station, originally built in 1846, had just been remodeled in the current year of 1883. Dignitaries, including the aging Emperor William I of Germany, were gathered to watch the newly installed direct current electric lighting system showcase the station. The flip of the switch turned out to be more dramatic than expected, however, and a large part of a wall was collapsed by a huge explosion, nearly taking William with it. Following this major malfunction and a series of other quality-control issues—light-bulbs were burning out as fast as they could be replaced—the talented Tesla was dispatched to see what he could do to repair the damage, both to the direct current system and the sensitivities of the Alsace people.

Upon arrival he realized that this was not merely a case of crossed wires; there were fundamental flaws in the direct current system design. Batchelor had been warning Edison that generators coming to Europe from America were defective—"fires from faulty armatures and poor insulation were becoming all too common."[37] According to Tesla, the wiring was defective and the explosion that took down the wall resulted from a massive short circuit.[38] Tesla took on the task of correcting the problem and spent nearly a year redesigning the generators and reinstalling the lighting system.

His year in Strasbourg was not all spent fixing the dynamo problems for Edison. When not at the rail station or challenging others to games of billiards, Tesla was diligently working on developing the alternating current induction motor that he had envisioned a year before in Budapest. Anticipating a lengthy stay, Tesla had brought with him some needed supplies and at a mechanical shop opposite the railroad station "undertook construction of a simple motor."[39]

By summer he "finally had the satisfaction of seeing rotation effected by alternating currents of different phase, and without sliding contacts or commutator."[40] Excited that he had finally put his vision into operation, Tesla enlisted the help of Mr. Bauzin, the Mayor of Strasbourg, who eagerly solicited some of the local wealthy elite as possible investors. To Tesla's mortification, the Mayor received no responses at all. Frustrated, Tesla made plans to return to Paris and hopefully to a better reception for his ideas.

So with the Strasbourg rail station now fully lit and accepted by the Alsace government, Tesla "returned to Paris with pleasing anticipations." Administrators at Edison's European works had promised Tesla "a liberal compensation" should he succeed in fixing the Strasbourg problem, "as well as fair consideration of the improvements [Tesla] had made in their dynamos." He, perhaps naively, hoped to "realize a substantial sum."[41] That sum was never to be realized.

The Edison men passed around non-decisions until Tesla finally recognized that his promised compensation was more rhetorical than realistic. While hugely disillusioned by how he had been treated, Tesla was simultaneously being pressed by Charles Batchelor to move to America, ostensibly to redesign and improve on the Edison dynamos and motors. Seeing an opportunity to present his alternating current designs directly to the great Thomas Edison himself, Tesla put aside his disappointment and agreed to make the cross-Atlantic voyage to the "land of the golden promise."[42]

Opposite: Thomas Edison

Though its actual existence is disputed,[43] O'Neill states that Batchelor penned a letter of introduction to Thomas Edison in which he stated simply: "I know two great men and you are one of them; the other is this young man."[44]

Tesla was off to America. But things were not to go exactly as planned.

(No Model.)

3 Sheets—Sheet 3.

N. TESLA.
DYNAMO ELECTRIC MACHINE.

Fig. 7.

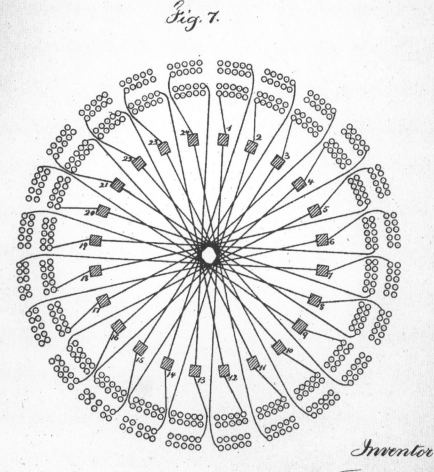

Witnesses

Chas. H. Smith
Geo. T. Pinckney

Inventor

Nikola Tesla

for Lemuel W. Serrell

Atty

THE ODD MR. TESLA

By the time Nikola Tesla moved to America he may or may not have already been considered a great man, but he was considered an eccentric—even peculiar—one. Oddities and idiosyncrasies were to become almost a trademark for him, though not by intention. But even Tesla had to admit that he was a bit odd, both by European and American standards. This started when he was very young.

Visions

In his boyhood Tesla suffered from what he called "his peculiar affliction."[1] Without warning, he would see images floating in his line of sight. Visualizing things is, of course, something that everybody experiences at one time or another. But to Tesla these visions were "often accompanied by strong flashes of light."[2] Simply hearing a spoken word would send the image of the object mentioned "vividly to my vision and sometimes I was quite unable to distinguish" whether what he saw was tangible or not. He often asked one of his sisters to tell him—was the object really there or merely his imagination? These visions would remain fixed in place even though he could "reach out and pass my hand through them."[3] Tesla suggested that his brother Dane had experienced similar troubles when he was alive.

In these visions he could even travel beyond his physical space, into other rooms, even other parts of the planet, despite having at this point in his life seen very little of the world.[4]

"Then I instinctively commenced to make excursions beyond the limits of the small world of which I had knowledge, and I saw new scenes. These were at first very blurred and indistinct, and would flit away when I tried to concentrate my attention upon them, but by and by I succeeded in fixing them; they gained in strength and distinctness and finally assumed the concreteness of real things. I soon discovered that my best comfort was attained if I simply went on in my vision farther and farther, getting new impressions all the time, and so I began to travel—of course, in my mind. Every night (and sometimes during the day), when alone, I would start on my journeys—see new places, cities and countries—live there, meet people and make friendships and acquaintances and, however unbelievable, it is a fact that they were just as dear to me as those in actual life and not a bit less intense in their manifestations."[5]

To some that might actually sound rather fun. But for now these visions and their accompanying flashes of light and sound caused Tesla "great discomfort and anxiety."[6] Much later, when he was about seventeen, he would learn to harness these visions to visualize his inventions "with the greatest facility" and turn his affliction into a benefit. He could picture the greatest machines in his mind without the need of models, drawings or experiments.[7]

Once Tesla became comfortable with his control of these visions he theorized about their possible cause. Reassuring himself that he was otherwise normal and not prone to "hallucinations such as are composed in diseased and anguished minds," Tesla came to believe these visions were "the result of a reflex action from the brain on the retina under great excitation." "If my explanation is correct," he would later say, "it should be possible to project on a screen the image of any object one conceives and make it visible. Such an advance would revolutionise [sic] all human relations. I am convinced that this wonder can and will be accomplished in time to come. I may add that I have devoted much thought to the solution of the problem."

It would be one of many problems to which Tesla "devoted much thought" in his ensuing career.

Exerting Self-Control

Before he could begin that new career, however, Tesla had to get control of these discomforting visions. His father had always been a practitioner and promoter of self-control. Besides having to conquer the visions and blinding flashes of light, Tesla felt that "up to the age of eight years, [his] character was weak and vacillating." He was "swayed by superstitious belief and lived in constant dread of the spirit of evil, of ghosts and ogres and other unholy monsters of the dark." He believed that he had "neither courage nor strength to form a firm resolve."

"My feelings came in waves and surges and vibrated unceasingly between extremes. My wishes were of consuming force and like the heads of the hydra, they multiplied. I was opprest by thoughts of pain in life and death and religious fear."[8]

And then "there came a tremendous change which altered the course of my whole existence."

Always someone who craved books (even to the extent of sneaking candles into his bedroom against his father's orders to read at night), he came across a novel when he was eight years old entitled *Abafi* (the Son of Aba). *Abafi* was a Serbian translation of a work by a well-known Hungarian writer. Much later, when Tesla reflected on the event, he

described the lessons of the author as "similar to those of Lew Wallace," a Union general in the U.S. Civil War who was better known for his historical novel, *Ben-Hur: A Tale of the Christ*, published in 1880.[9] *Abafi* wakened his "dormant powers of will" and allowed Tesla to begin to practice self-control.[10] In short, he was training his mind to focus on the task at hand. "At first my resolutions faded like snow in April," he noted in his autobiography, "but in a little while I conquered my weakness and felt a pleasure I never knew before—that of doing as I willed. In the course of time this vigorous mental exercise became second nature."

This self-control was not so easy at first. Long before he was even twenty years old he smoked excessively—"fifteen or twenty big black cigars every day"[11]—and later "contracted a mania for gambling."[12] In the case of the smoking it was his ailing younger sister that begged him to stop, and he did, never to smoke again. He also at that time discovered that his periodic heart trouble was due to the innocent cup of coffee he consumed every morning. He claimed he "discontinued at once," although also confessed "it was not an easy task."[13]

"In this way I checked and bridled other habits and passions and have not only preserved my life but derived an immense amount of satisfaction from what most men would consider privation and sacrifice."[14]

The gambling was more problematic to overcome. His father abhorred the "senseless waste" of time and money, to which Nikola merely claimed (as do most enthusiasts) that "I can stop whenever I please" while ignoring Milutin's anger and contempt. His mother, more insightfully, tried a different approach, handing him a roll of bills and telling him, "the sooner you lose all we possess, the better it will be. I know that you will get over it." Nikola put an end to his addiction "then and there . . . tearing it from his heart so as not to leave even a trace of desire."

Opposite: Tesla in 1885, at age twenty-nine, shortly after his arrival in the United States

No Sex for Nikola

Not leaving a trace of desire apparently extended to his sexuality. Tesla scholar Marc Seifer, cites William H. Terbo (the son of Tesla's sister's son) as suggesting that "womanizing" may have contributed in part to Tesla never completing his studies in Graz.[15] Yet despite the opinion of a professional palmist, who opined that Tesla's hand revealed "a flirtatious streak," Tesla purposefully chose celibacy.[16] This did not stop the media of the time (even the technical journals) from urging him to get married— after all, "important people were expected to procreate for the good of the country."[17] As young science writer and close friend Kenneth Swezey later put it, "Tesla's only marriage has been to his work and to the world . . . he believes . . . that the most enduring works of achievement have come from childless men . . . "[18] Swezey described Tesla as "an absolute celibate."[19] Tesla himself claimed that to be a great inventor one must not allow himself to be distracted by love. When asked if he believed in marriage he replied that:

"for an artist, yes; for a musician, yes; for a writer, yes; but for an inventor, no. The first three must gain inspiration from a woman's influence and be led by their love to finer achievement, but an inventor has so intense a nature with so much in it of wild, passionate quality, that in giving himself to a woman he might love, he would give everything, and so take everything from his chosen field. I do not think you can name many great inventions that have been made by married men."[20]

Oddities Abound

But these characteristics were, at least to some extent, intentionally chosen by Tesla. Other traits were well beyond anything that could be written off as the eccentricities of a genius. In his autobiography Tesla admits that over the years he had "contracted many strange likes, dislikes and habits":

"I had a violent aversion against the earrings of women but other ornaments, as bracelets, pleased me more or less according to design. The sight of a pearl would almost give me a fit but I was fascinated with the glitter of crystals or objects with sharp edges and plane surfaces. I would not touch the hair of other people except, perhaps, at the point of a revolver. I would get a fever by looking at a peach and if a piece of camphor was anywhere in the house it caused me the keenest discomfort."[21]

It did not stop there. He gave up drinking coffee and tea. He developed the habit of counting the steps in the long 8–10 mile walks he would take around New York City. While he dined at the fanciest of restaurants—often Delmonico's steak house—he would calculate "the cubical contents of soup plates, coffee cups and pieces of food." Not doing so would take all the enjoyment out of the meal. The waiters at Delmonico's knew to always provide him with eighteen napkins since, according to Tesla, "all repeated acts or operations I performed had to be divisible by three." Missing count meant that he "felt impelled to do it all over again, even if it took hours."

Above: Delmonico's, New York, ca. 1903

Mr. Tesla Explains Why He Will Never Marry

Famous Scientist Felt Unworthy of Woman as She Used To Be, and Now H[e] Can't Endure Her Trying to Outdo the Men

Mrs. Davenport Engberg, the director of a symphony orchestra and a good example of the way women are entering fields that used to be exclusively man's

Ida Schnall, the all-round woman athlete, in a boxing bout with Willie Bradley—a sure indication, according to Mr. Tesla's rather gloomy views, that our civilization is deteriorating

Nikola Tesla, the electrical wizard whose discoveries paved the way for this radio age

Renee Prahar, one of many women who are trying to outstrip the men in sculpture

A woman worker in a Michigan railroad machine shop

"In place of the soft voiced, gentle woman of my reverent worship," Mr. Tesla, "has come the woman who thinks that her chief success in life lies in making herself as much as possible like man—in dress, voice and actions, in sports and achievements of every kind"

WHEN a man who has made a name for himself deliberately chooses to remain a bachelor the world is naturally curious to know what the reasons were that impelled him to this choice.

Marriage has come to be considered the natural thing for every normal man, and when some pre-eminent man shows a firm determination to sidestep it everybody wonders whether his superior intelligence has revealed to him some fatal defects in the institution of matrimony which are not apparent to the average person.

But the public's curiosity in this respect is seldom gratified. Most of the distinguished bachelors try to pass off their bachelorhood as a joke, saying that it is not a matter of choice, but because they have never been able to find a woman who would marry them. As a rule, they are singularly averse to giving any serious reasons for their failure to become husbands.

Nikola Tesla, the great scientist and inventor, is a striking exception to this rule. In a recent interview with a representative of this newspaper he frankly explains why he has never married and why he probably never will marry.

And in connection with his explanation he presents some ideas about woman's freedom and what he thinks it is sure to lead to that will be read with interest by those who agree with him as well as by the many who will not.

In the past the reason why Mr. Tesla never married was because his estimation of woman placed her on such a lofty pedestal that he could never bring himself to feel worthy of her. Now that she has, as he feels, stepped down from her pedestal and bettered all her noblest qualities for what is called her "freedom," he is even more disinclined to matrimony than he was before.

Although of course Mr. Tesla is too gallant a gentleman to say it in so many words, his comments led it to be inferred that he thinks the new woman almost as far beneath him as the one of other days was above him. Accordingly in his views, the sex has rushed from one extreme to another of quite a different kind, and in the plunge it has left for Mr. Tesla and other bachelors who think as he does no "happy medium" such as Josiah Allen's wife used to declare one of the essentials to happiness.

"I had always thought of woman," says Mr. Tesla, "as possessing those delicate qualities of mind and soul that made her in these respects far superior to man. I had put her on a lofty pedestal, figuratively speaking, and ranked her in certain important attributes considerably higher than man. I worshiped at the feet of the creature I had raised to this height, and, like every true worshiper, I felt myself unworthy of the object of my worship.

"But all this was in the past. Now the soft-voiced gentlewoman of my reverent worship has all but vanished. In her place has come the woman who thinks that her chief success in life lies in making herself as much as possible like man—in dress, voice and actions, in sports and achievements of every kind."

In these words the great electrical genius sums up the reasons for his bachelorhood.

Some who read them will urge that his view of womankind is distorted by the years he has spent in the laboratory, dealing with inanimate things and developing perhaps an abnormal shyness which acts as an insuperable barrier to marriage. Others will say that the very fact of his detachment from the ordinary routine of life makes him all the better qualified to point out its defects and to criticize the change for the worse which he believes new conditions have brought to womankind.

"Women," says Mr. Tesla, "are becoming stronger than men, both physically and mentally.

"The world has experienced many tragedies, but to my mind the greatest tragedy of all is the present economic condition wherein women strive against men, and in many cases actually succeed in usurping their places in the professions and in industry. This growing tendency of women to overshadow the masculine is a sign of a deteriorating civilization.

"Woman's determined competition with man in the business world is breaking down some of the best traditions—things which have proved the moving factors in the world's slow but substantial progress.

"Practically all the great achievements of man until now have been inspired by his love and devotion to woman. Man has aspired to great things because some woman believed in him, because he wished to command her admiration and respect. For these reasons he has fought for her and risked his life and his all for her time and time again.

"Perhaps the male in human society is useless. I am frank to admit that I don't know. If women are beginning to feel this way about it—and there is striking evidence at hand that they do—then we are entering upon the cruelest period of the world's history.

"Our civilization will sink to a state like that which is found among the bees, ants and other insects—a state wherein the male is ruthlessly killed off. In this matriarchal empire which will be established the female rules. As the female predominates, the males are at her mercy. The male is considered important only as a factor in the general scheme of the continuity of life.

"The tendency of women to push aside man, supplanting the old spirit of co-operation with him in all the affairs of life, is very disappointing to me.

"Women's independence and her cleverness in obtaining what she wants in the business world is breaking down man's spirit of independence. The old fire he once experienced at being able to achieve something that would compel and hold a woman's devotion is turning to ashes.

"It seems to me that anything which adds to the great discontent which we observe on every side to-day must be bad influence on our life. Women who keep themselves agitated by their tre-

"Women don't seem to want that sort of thing to-day. They appear to want to control and govern. They want man to look up to them, instead of their looking up to him."

Mr. Tesla is not given to making statements that he cannot prove. His life's work has been based on logic, not on excess.

In voicing his gloomy views of modern life Mr. Tesla says his observations are not confined to the women of this country. Conditions abroad, he says, suggest that the same tendency is worldwide. Having always regarded woman as a super-being, he expresses great sadness over the change he thinks the last few years have brought in her.

"I am considering this question not merely from the standpoint of a man," he points out. "I am thinking of the woman's side of it.

"As we contemplate any change, we naturally take into consideration the results that may follow such an innovation. One of the results to my mind is quite a pathetic one. Woman, herself, is really the victim instead of, as she thinks, the victor. Contentment is absent from her life. She is ambitious, often far beyond her natural equipment, to attain the thing she wants. She too frequently forgets that all women cannot be prima donnas and motion picture stars.

"Woman's discontent makes the life of the present day still more overstressed. The high pitch given to existence by people who are restless and dissatisfied because they fail to achieve things wholly out of proportion to the health and talent with which Nature has endowed them is a bad thing for the world.

"It seems to me that women are not particularly happy in this newly found freedom, in this new competition which they are waging so persistently against men in business and the professions and even in sport. The question that naturally arises is, whether the women themselves are the gainers or the losers.

"Discontent makes for cranks and unnatural people. There seems to be an uncommon number of them about to-day. This is one of the reasons I remain apart from the crowd. The public, or semi-public, character is the target for all sorts of attacks and unpleasant communications.

"For example, I used to receive all sorts of strange notes, many of them letters from cranks threatening my life, because they had read about my experiments in manufacturing lightning bolts. They wrote that they believed I was using these lightning flashes to kill them!

"The 'power of the true woman is so great that I believe if a beautiful woman—that is to say, one beautiful in spirit, in manner and in thought, in a goddess—tries to appear suddenly on earth, she could command the whole world. Her leadership, I believe, would be universally recognized.

"History has given us many cases of the wonderful influence exercised by unusual women. Among these have been the mothers of great men. But the influence lay not in their determination to outdo men, or even to compete with him.

"Perhaps because woman is a far more highly sensitized instrument she knows by instinct her power understands that the extent of it lies the high position she takes for herself that the superior never descends to level of the commonplace."

These views of Nikola Tesla will received with great interest, whether one agrees or not with his idea that is going to pull down to ruin whole social structure. He is generally recognized as one of the greatest authorities of the present day.

Twenty years ago Tesla astonished the world by flashing a wireless message clear around the globe. His engineering mental work paved the way for the age in which we are now living.

These views of Nikola Tesla will received with great interest, whether one agrees or not with his idea that to be quickly and economically admitted to any desired part of the earth—and, perhaps, some day to Mars other planets.

Some philosopher has said that is perilous for a man to say he never marry as for a physician to predict the exact hour of a patient death. Mr. Tesla is not an old man. Perhaps he will live long enough to some woman who will be able to convince him that she has attained her freedom without sacrificing any of womanly qualities which he so greatly admires.

When walking home at night he would walk around the block three times.[22] Upon arriving in Colorado Springs (on May 18) he stayed in room 207 (divisible by three) and left instructions to the maid to deliver eighteen clean towels daily (an odd request but given that Tesla tipped well, one that the maid accommodated cheerily).[23]

This "cerebral cinema" was something for which Tesla did daily exercises; all the better to develop better introspection.[24] Supposedly these exercises, which most people today might call obsessive-compulsive disorder (OCD), would put him into a meditative state that, according to Tesla, would be the foundations of his inventions. In a letter to the *New York Times* Tesla stated:

"[I] would prefer to qualify original investigation or research, discovery, and invention as 'creative' scientific effort, which is equivalent to that of the artist, though it springs from a different, if not opposite, motive."

Tesla went on arguing rather metaphysically:

"Both the artist and man of science are striving for independence from the material world in the only two ways possible—one by its casting off, the other by its complete mastery."[25]

This obsessive-compulsiveness, which would become more pronounced as he aged, showed signs early in his academic career. For example, when Tesla was at the Institute of Technology at Graz, he "had a veritable mania for finishing whatever I began." Once, after he started to read the works of Voltaire, he learned "to his dismay" that there were

Opposite: *Galveston Daily News*, 1924

close to one hundred large volumes in small print "which that monster had written while drinking seventy-two cups of black coffee per diem." Obsessed with finishing—"it had to be done"—Tesla got through every volume and then declared to himself that he would "never more" take on such a chore.[26]

Tesla remained a night person all of his life, getting by on as little as three hours of sleep and sometimes going for a few days with nothing more than catnaps. To the consternation of some of his assistants, Tesla's routine would be to arrive at his laboratory "promptly at noon."[27] His secretary would be required to meet him at the door to take his hat, cane, and gloves. Tesla often spoke to himself while working, talking through the questions only he could understand. During lightning storms the shades would be raised on the otherwise closed-up room so that Tesla could be inspired by the flashes of light that mimicked his own namesake coil. At these times, according to his assistants, Tesla's self-talk became "positively eloquent."

Sometimes these oddities would take on an unkind flare. Tesla was always thin, so much so that in later years he would often be considered gaunt, even skeletal. Perhaps because of his own lifelong scarcity of fat he was intolerant of those whom he felt were overweight. He was disgusted by obese people and would avoid them whenever possible.[28] O'Neill put it this way:

"He also had clear-cut ideas about the feminine figure. He disliked the big "hefty" type and utterly detested fat women. The super-upholstered type, flashily dressed and heavily jeweled, that wasted time in hotel lobbies, were his pet abomination. He liked women trim, slim, graceful and agile."[29]

Along with this aversion for portliness, Tesla was fastidious in his daily dress, even when in the laboratory. His usual street attire "included a Prince Albert coat and a derby hat . . . his handkerchiefs were of white silk rather than linen, his neckties sober, and his collars stiff."[30] These were replaced frequently. With this persnickety manner, it is perhaps not surprising that Tesla was known to criticize the clothing choices of his assistants and secretaries, once forcing a secretary to go home and change before delivering a message to an important banker.[31] The woman, who was "well proportioned," had worn a dress that was "in the very latest style," with an extremely low waistline that resulted in a relatively short skirt, which "from the neck to the hips . . . was almost a plain cylinder."[32] She had made it herself and was very proud of both her style and her talent as a seamstress. Tesla, however, was not impressed:

"Miss," he said, "what is that you are wearing? You cannot wear that on this errand on which I wish you to go. I wished to have you take a note to a very important banker down town, and what would he think if someone from my office should come to him wearing such a monstrosity of a gown? How can you be such a slave to fashion? . . . Now, Miss, you get into a cab, so not many people will see you, and go to your home and get into a sensible dress and return as soon as you can so you can take this letter down town for me."[33]

O'Neill also notes that Tesla never addressed any of his female employees by their actual names, either their given or surnames. He would simply call them "Miss." Worse, with his heavy European accent it would come out as "Meese." When he wanted to express his severe dissatisfaction, as in the case with the secretary he was berating, he would stretch it out to sound like "Meeeeeeeesssse." Said as such, according to O'Neill, who witnessed this in person, it could be "an abrupt, abbreviated expletive."[34]

Germs Be Gone

Tesla was also germaphobic. Before eating he would use one of his eighteen napkins to gently wipe the germs off of each piece of silverware, china and glassware.[35] He commonly wore fine leather gloves and refused to shake hands with anyone. On the rare occasions that he was unable to avoid a handshake he would quickly excuse himself and rush off to the washroom to cleanse the offending germs off his hand. Prone to idiosyncratic behavior, Tesla's fear of germs began after he observed through a microscope the many microscopic creatures found in normal drinking water. About the experience Tesla would later write to Robert Underwood Johnson, "If you would watch only for a few minutes the horrible creatures, hairy and ugly beyond anything you can conceive, tearing each other up with the juices diffusing throughout the water—you would never again drink a drop of unboiled or unsterilized water."[36]

A Peculiar Passion for Pigeons

Despite his rampant fear of germs, Tesla did not seem to mind mingling with the pigeons that inhabited the Bryant Park area near his laboratory. The fact that he liked the birds was not necessarily odd; he had after all grown up in a country village surrounded by "pigeons, chickens and sheep, and our magnificent flock of geese which used to rise to the clouds in the morning and return from the feeding grounds at sundown

Above: Tesla's closest friends
Opposite: *Salt Lake Herald*, June 27, 1897

STRANGEST MAN IN NEW YORK.

Nikola Tesla and His Perpetual Motion Machine.

New York, June 25.—The strangest man in this city is unquestionably Nikola Tesla. Within the past fortnight he has astounded scientists the world over by his announcement that he had perfected his wireless telegraph—in other words, that he had sent and received communications between distant points without the use of wires and simply by employing the natural energy of the earth. Nature, he says, teems with power and motion.

Tesla is a young man. He has just passed his fortieth birthday. If he lives 20 years or more and retains his faculties the world will be a different place to live in compared with today. His ideas and projects are so big that it

ing." So Tesla does not gamble now, at least, not over the card table. His laboratory supplies all the excitement that his emotion can stand.

Tesla's father was a clergyman of the Greek church, and it was intended that the son should fit himself for the same life. The idea of entering the ministry was opposed by the boy with such pertinacity that at last his father compromised by agreeing that he should become a professor of mathematics and physics. With that end in view Tesla was sent to the Polytechnic Institute at Gratz, and there, in operation, was a gramme dynamo. That simple electrical instrument, the first that he had seen, settled the feature calling of Tesla.

Prior to entering the Polytechnic at Gratz he had first attended a public

tion of them made the leading French electricians regard their originator as a fanciful dreamer. Some friend advised him to come to America. This he did, and, hunting up Thomas A. Edison, soon convinced that genius that he was a valuable man to employ.

Tesla's stay with Edison was brief. He had his own ideas, and, it is believed, they clashed with Edison's. Tesla has never said much about this. Right here it should be mentioned that the Montenegrans has not the jealousy common among inventors. He never belittles the work of any man, and he has done more for young electricians just starting out than any other dozen men of his profession.

       GRANTLAND GRIEVE.

HE GOT THEM BOTH.

The Fledgling Lawyer Makes a Splendid Stroke of Business.

Detroit Free Press: "My best stroke of business was when I first hung out my shingle in the west," told the lawyer who now handles none but the most important and remunerative cases. "Living about 50 miles north of the town in which I was impatiently waiting for something to do, was an eccentric old fellow who owned enough land to make three or four counties and enough cattle to feed the armies of the world.

"As I was pacing up and down the little office one morning, wondering what I could go at if my first case didn't come soon, I answered a knock at the door to meet a young lady who had all the glow and vigor of the prairie with the easy society ways of the cultured eastern woman. While I was trying to recover my breath she told me that she was a messenger from her father, who had heard that there was a new lawyer in town, and wanted his opinion in a matter that threatened to lead to a lawsuit. I took the letter she handed me and found it signed by the rich old ranchman.

" 'But your father asks an opinion without making any statement of his case,' I said after reading.

" 'It's evident that you don't know papa. If you sent back for further information he would denounce you as an ignoramus and have nothing more to do with you. Write something learned in language but obscure in ideas. Quote a lot of your musty old legal maxims in the original Latin, and, above all things, abuse the other man with merciless bitterness.'

"In three hours she was back from her shopping, and the 'learned opinion' was ready. The language was ponderous. The sentences were long and involved. The Latin was injected without reference to the context, and the abuse was underlined with red ink. She read and laughed till her sparkling eyes rained tears down her brilliant cheeks. 'You must arrange to do all papa's law business,' she warned me at parting, and I danced a boisterous solo when she was gone.

"Next day came a letter from 'papa.' He had at last found a lawyer. That opinion was worthy of a Webster or a Choate. He enclosed $1,000, and made me his attorney. Later I got the daughter."

Rapid Stenography.

Washington Post: Anent the prevailing discussions as to the highest speed ever attained by expert shorthand writers here is a story going the rounds of the seat of a Georgia court stenographer, which by long odds broke the world's record in that line of work.

It was when that eminent jurist, the late Judge Richard Clark, was presiding in the Atlanta circuit of the superior court. One of the most remarkable murder trials was in progress. The evidence was conflicting and the judge was called upon to charge the jury on some decidedly new and interesting legal points. Now the judge was a rapid talker. In this instance it was very important that every word he spoke should be correctly recorded, and he so cautioned the stenographer.

Then Judge Clarke began. As he warmed up to his charge he was speaking at the rate of 250 words a minute,

in battle formation."[37] He marveled at how these birds could "put a squadron of the best aviators of the present day to shame."[38]

When he was six years old and moved from the tiny village of Smiljan to the still not very large city of Gospić he experienced a "calamity" that almost broke his heart—he had to leave his bird and beast friends behind. He felt a prisoner in his new house, afraid to go out and meet the more brash "city dudes." He would rather face a "roaring lion."[39] This fear of the city was only heightened when, in a bit of unfortunate timing, after ringing the church bells and racing down the steps, he accidentally ripped the sweeping train off the dress of "a good but pompous woman," resulting in the only (albeit mild) corporal punishment he ever received from his father. Tesla would later relate in his memoir that his embarrassment and confusion were "indescribable."

Whether these childhood traumas led to his fascination with pigeons later in life is hard to know. Despite always dressing impeccably, Tesla nonetheless could be occasionally found standing in Bryant Park, arms outstretched, bird feed at his feet, and covered in pigeons. He was a sight to behold, and passersby chuckled at the idea of the great scientist enamored of what most would agree are not the cleanest or most

Above: Tesla's favorite white pigeon
Opposite: The first practical telautomaton

appealing of birds. But here he was . . . mingling with the feisty fowl just steps from his scientific laboratory.

On other occasions Tesla would wander the streets of New York City, head down, gazing intently, on the alert for the injured pigeon that mistook the windowed glass of the slowly rising skyscrapers of New York for a passageway (or a possible mate, one might imagine). Rushing to any bird he observed, Tesla gently lifted his newfound charge and brought it back to his hotel room to nurse it back to health.

Perhaps the most bizarre event related to his pigeon fanaticism was on the night he received the Edison Medal. Originated in 1909 by the AIEE, the Edison Medal is given "for a career of meritorious achievement in electrical science, electrical engineering or the electrical arts." While named in honor of the great inventor, Thomas Edison actually has nothing to do with the award.[40] It is, however, the oldest and most coveted medal in the field of engineering in the United States.[41] Prior to Tesla it had been awarded only six times; recipients up to that point included such eminent icons as Alexander Graham Bell and George Westinghouse.

So it was on such an esteemed occasion that Tesla was nowhere to be found in the room when the time came to award the medal. Granted, Tesla was not exactly thrilled with the idea of getting a medal named for his arch-rival in the first place, but it was a bit odd to run out on receiving a prestigious award, even for someone as odd as Tesla. Frantic, Bernard Behrend, who had been the one to talk him into receiving the medal, finding no one in the restrooms or anterooms, sprinted outside the 40th Street building housing the Engineers Club, which wasn't far from the famous New York Public Library. Remembering the many walks Tesla

Above: Edison Medal
Opposite: Bryant Park, New York City

would take in Bryant Park to feed the pigeons, Behrend hurried down the street to the library. And there, on the steps between the imposing marble lions guarding the library, was one of the most bizarre scenes he could imagine.[42]

There was Tesla, "his height exaggerated by the streamlined contours of his swallow-tailed formal evening dress," standing in a large circle of observers and "wearing a crown of two pigeons on his head, his shoulders and arms festooned with a dozen more, their white or pale-blue bodies making strong contrast with his black suit and black hair." If this sight was not odd enough, "on either of his outstretched hands was another bird, while seemingly hundreds more made a living carpet on the ground in front of him, hopping about and pecking at the bird seed he had scattered."[43]

Eventually, Behrend would return with Tesla to the auditorium of the Engineers Club so Tesla could receive his Edison Medal. But Tesla's fascination with pigeons continued to the end of his life. Such an odd paradox was this man. Desperately germophobic to the point of avoiding human contact, here he was covered in bird feathers ... and worse. And when he took ill and could not tend to his rounds, he would order his assistants to go out looking for injured pigeons in his stead. Given careful

Opposite: Tesla in his laboratory, lighting a disconnected vacuum bulb by high-frequency currents, 1898

instructions on where to look and how to handle the birds, they were to bring them back and care for them if Tesla could not.

Odd to the End

A notoriously poor sleeper, often getting no more than an hour or so nap at a time, Tesla also would periodically take what could only be referred to as "electric baths." He had done this with full showman skills at the Chicago World's Fair and during many demonstrations since then. Placing himself on an insulated platform of hard rubber, he would start up his induction coil (Tesla coil). Approaching the free terminal with a metallic object in his hand to avoid burns, Tesla would transmit millions of volts per second through and around his body. Unseen streamers of electricity would cover his body, creating "a sensation like the pricking of a needle." By reaching out with his fingers toward the coil, long sparks would bridge the gap in streams of light. "The streamers offer no particular inconvenience," Tesla would claim, "except that in the ends of the finger tips [sic] a burning sensation is felt."[44] In fact, Tesla found these treatments to be exhilarating and cleansing.

In the last decade of his life Tesla became even more reclusive than usual, rarely leaving his rooms in the New Yorker Hotel other than to make his now fairly regular pigeon reconnaissance missions. Out of money—the cost of the rooms was being covered by the Westinghouse company—Tesla began subsisting on only milk and Nabisco crackers.[45] With his few remaining friends dying off, Tesla was visited only by the much younger writer Kenneth Swezey and a former employee, Charles Hauser, the latter of whom usually took care of Tesla's pigeons when Tesla was too frail to do so himself.

All of these idiosyncrasies would make him an interesting man to behold in both the negative and positive sense of the phrase.

No. 787,412.

PATENTED APR. 18, 1905.

N. TESLA.
ART OF TRANSMITTING ELECTRICAL ENERGY THROUGH THE NATURAL MEDIUMS.

APPLICATION FILED MAY 16, 1900. RENEWED JUNE 17, 1902.

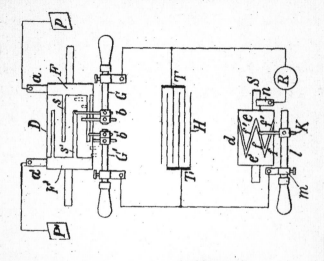

Fig. 2

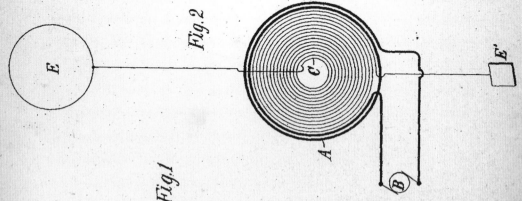

Fig. 1

Witnesses:
Raphaël Netter
M. Lawson Dyer.

Nikola Tesla   Inventor
by Ker. Page & Cooke Att'ys

CHAPTER
AMPERE
4

OF EDISON AND WESTING- HOUSE

rriving in America after a less than perfect Atlantic crossing—his money had been stolen and a small mutiny had
occurred en route[1]—Tesla was eager to develop his alternating current system. His first impressions of New York City when he
arrived in 1884, however, were less than complimentary. After living a
cultured life in the capitals of Europe, Tesla was shocked at what he
found in this new continent's largest city:

"What I had left was beautiful, artistic and
fascinating in every way; what I saw here was machined,
rough and unattractive."[2]

Later he would find solace cavorting with the fashionably dressed,
better-off elites on Fifth Avenue. The entry point for all immigrants,
however, was still the Castle Garden Depot—Ellis Island would not open
for another eight years and the Statue of Liberty was still standing in Paris.
Overall, things were not great in America when Tesla arrived. The

country was going through one of its periodic downturns. The Wall Street stock exchange had crashed in the spring and the ensuing panic led to the bankruptcy of three major banks and thousands of companies. There was some hope as things seemed to be getting better, but new immigrants were not always welcome as they were perceived as taking from Americans some of the few jobs available.[3] The land of the golden promise might offer opportunities, but success was not a guarantee.[4] This is the New York City to which Nikola Tesla arrived—dangerous, loud, and dirty.

While accounts differ as to whether Tesla visited a friend and helped out a mechanic before heading down to the Pearl Street generating station, he did quickly meet the famed Thomas Edison. Tesla was apparently impressed with the man whom a newspaper reporter would later dub "The Wizard of Menlo Park."[5] Tesla remembered:

"The meeting with Edison was a memorable event in my life. I was amazed at this wonderful man who, without early advantages and scientific training, had accomplished so much."

Above: Castle Garden
Opposite: The Panic of 1884

Edison, in contrast, was not so impressed with the twenty-eight-year-old Serb. Though only thirty-seven years old himself, Edison had already built an empire in his Menlo Park (now Edison), New Jersey, laboratories. His inventions included improvements on the telegraph, development of the first commercially practical incandescent light, longer lasting lightbulbs, and the earliest versions of his phonograph. His greatest invention was the development of the direct current power system that allowed electricity generation and distribution to businesses and wealthy homeowners.

With all of these to his name already, Edison's initial view of Tesla was as a rather pretentious newcomer with wild ideas. Tesla encouraged this view by immediately declaring that his own polyphase system was superior to the direct current system and "was the only practical kind of current to use in a power-and-lighting system."[6] Edison laughed off this suggestion. Not only had he already rejected the alternating current system as too dangerous and lacking in key elements, he had also invested his company entirely in the development and sales of direct current. Still, Edison decided to give Tesla a job doing largely routine repair work.

That changed when a crisis emerged on the steamship S.S. *Oregon*. One of the fastest and most modern passenger ships of the time, the *Oregon* was equipped with one of Edison's direct current lighting plants. Except it was not working. Both electrical generators, also called dynamos, had mysteriously failed and the ship was stranded in the port of New York until they could be repaired. Worse, the superstructure of the ship had been completed after the installation of the dynamos so they could not be simply pulled out and replaced. Edison, embarrassed and desperate, sent off the newly hired Tesla to see what he could do.

Tesla packed up the necessary instruments and boarded the vessel in the evening, discovering that "the dynamos were in bad condition, having several short-circuits and breaks." With the help of the *Oregon*'s crew, Tesla worked through the night and "succeeded in putting them in good shape."[7] At five the next morning he was heading back to the shop and ran into Edison and Batchelor. "Here is our Parisian running around at night," said Edison when spotting Tesla, who proceeded to tell him that both dynamos on the ship had been successfully repaired. According to Tesla, Edison simply looked at him in silence, then turned and walked away. "But when he had gone some distance I heard him

remark: 'Batchelor, this is a damn good man.'"

This incident raised Tesla's stock in Edison's eyes and henceforth Tesla "had full freedom in directing the work."[8] The work was interesting and Tesla was happy. Always the hard worker, for nearly a year Tesla regularly worked from 10:30 a.m. to five o'clock the next morning, seven days a week. Edison was duly impressed, saying, "I have had many hard-working assistants but you take the cake."[9] Tesla occasionally dined with Edison and other key leaders in Edison's various companies. Sometimes they would shoot billiards, where Tesla "would impress the fellows with his bank shots and vision of the future."[10]

Previous: (left) Thomas Edison, (right) S.S. *Oregon*

Seeing opportunities to improve Edison's dynamos, Tesla outlined a plan, stressing the output and cost efficiency of his intended changes. Edison, perhaps in a temporarily charitable moment, promised Tesla $50,000 if he could accomplish the task. Tesla immediately set to work and over the next year he designed twenty-four different types of dynamos, "eliminating the long-core field magnets then in use and substituting the more efficient short cores" as well as introducing some automatic controls.[11] The financial benefits to the Edison operations were enormous, but when Tesla demanded payment, Edison's response was to laugh and say, "You are still a Parisian. When you become a full-fledged American, you will appreciate an American joke."[12]

Tesla, feeling "a painful shock" at being cheated once again by Edison, immediately resigned. It was the spring of 1885.

By this time Tesla had developed a reputation as both a hard worker and an innovator. Quickly approached by two investors—B.A. Vail and Robert Lane—in March of 1885 they together founded the "Tesla Electric Light and Manufacturing Company." Tesla was most interested in developing his alternating current system; Vail and Lane were most interested in developing better arc lights for street and factory illumination. With his alternating current system once again put on the back burner, Tesla started work on improving arc lights.

1. Double Lamp.—2. Carbons.—3. Single Lamp.—4. Focusing Lamp.—5. Head-light Lamp.—6. Dial Attachment to Machine.—7. Ornamental Lamp.

Arc lighting is fundamentally different from that powered by both the direct and alternating current systems. Artificial luminescence is created by running an electrical current across a small gap between two carbon rods (today the rods are tungsten).[13] The current agitates the gas (for example neon, argon, xenon, mercury), which then fluoresces. The common fluorescent lamp of today is a kind of low-pressure mercury-arc lamp, although mostly these have been relegated to a few specialty uses such as the xenon-arc lamp used in IMAX projection systems.[14]

Above: Tesla's Egg of Columbus—a copper egg in a rotating magnetic field

At the time, however, arc lamps were still the main system for factory and municipal lighting. Within about a year after setting up the company, Tesla had patented an improved arc lamp that suppressed the disagreeable "flickering or hissing."[15]

Happy with the results and excited to move on to his alternating current system, Tesla was shocked to find out that his associates were not at all interested. In "the hardest blow I ever received," he was forced out of his own company with no other possession than "a beautifully engraved certificate of stock of hypothetical value." Once again Tesla had been cheated out of a job.[16]

The next year was one of the lowest points in Tesla's life. From the spring of 1886 to the winter of 1887 he worked as a day laborer, desperately competing with other unemployed men for any job he could find. "I lived through a year of terrible heartaches and bitter tears," he lamented, "my suffering being intensified by material want."[17] Tesla even resorted to being a ditch digger for $2 a day to put food on the table. He resented his wasted education and experience, grumbling despondently that "my high education in various branches of science, mechanics and literature seemed to me like a mockery."[18]

Above: Tesla's Egg of Columbus experiment as seen at the 1893 World's Columbian Exposition

Eventually he was able to impress the foreman of the work gang, who was captivated by Tesla's ever-optimistic stories of how his alternating current system would change electricity generation for all mankind. Tesla was introduced to prominent engineer Albert Brown and distinguished lawyer Charles Peck. Unlike the foreman, Peck was not so impressed with alternating current, at least until Tesla entertained him with his Egg of Columbus. The "Egg" refers to a legend in which Christopher Columbus tells fellow diners that he can stand an egg on its end. After watching with amusement as the others try to overcome the laws of physics, Columbus simply chips the shell slightly on one end and stands it upright to the astonished snickers of the dinner guests. Tesla's egg would likewise astonish Peck and Brown. He cast an egg in iron and brass, then, on their next meeting, put the egg on its side in the center of a circular enclosure constructed using polyphase circuits. As the current made the egg spin it eventually reached a speed at which it stood up on its tip like a top. This simple experiment allowed Tesla to suitably impress the two with the principles of his rotating magnetic field.[19]

SCIENTIFIC AMERICAN

September 30,

296

The top half of casings is removed, showing two rotors. Each rotor consists of 25 disks ⅛-inch thick by 18 inch diameter. The steam enters at the periphery, and flows in spiral paths to exhaust at the center disks. The driving turbine is to the left, the brake turbine to the right. Between them is a torsion spring. The steam inlets are on opposite sides on the two rotors; the driving rotor moving clockwise. The torsion of the spring is automatically shown by beams of light and mirrors and the horse-power is read off a scale. At 9,000 revolutions per minute, with 125 pounds at the throttle and free exhaust, this turbine develops 200 horse-power. It weighs two pounds per horse-power.

The Tesla turbine testing plant at the Edison Waterside Station, New York.

The Tesla Steam Turbine
The Rotary Heat Motor Reduced to Its Simplest Terms

output of 200 horse-power from a single-s

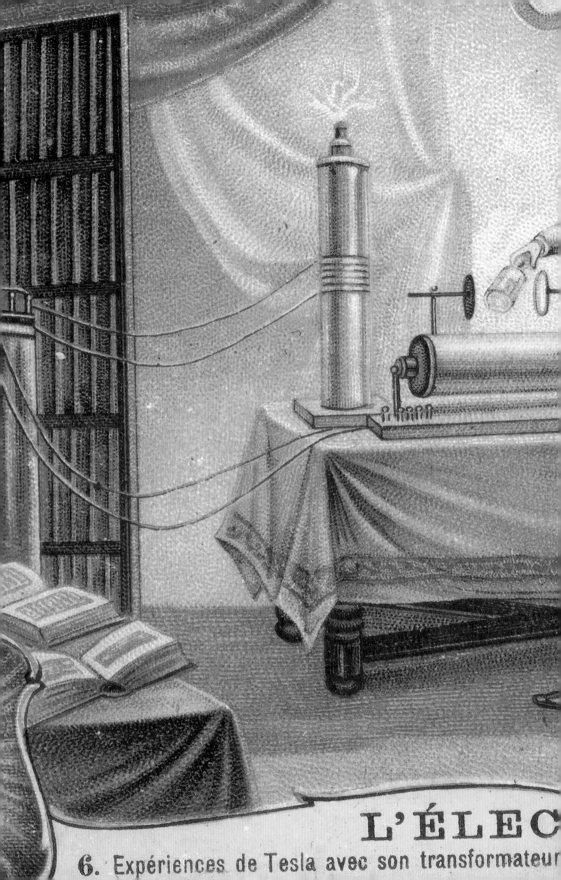

L'ÉLEC

6. Expériences de Tesla avec son transformateur

RICITÉ.

uisant la lumière au moyen de l'électricité (1895).

Soon afterwards, Peck and Brown joined Tesla in creating the Tesla Electric Company, with their first of many patents filed in the spring of 1887. Tesla was ecstatic. Not only did he finally have secure financing, but he now had a new well-equipped laboratory at 89 Liberty Street. Tesla was starting the most prolific period of invention in his life. Over the next decade and a half, Tesla would develop at least the basics of nearly every major discovery he would become known for in the future.[20]

Mostly working alone, or with his old friend Anton Szigeti who had by then joined him in New York, Tesla developed not only a single-phase alternating current system, but also a two- and three-phase system.[21] At first he built his new rotating magnetic field motors from the memories he had in his head, beginning with that first revelation in the park in Budapest. "The motors I built there were exactly as I had imagined them," he would say. "I made no attempt to improve the design, but merely reproduced the pictures as they appeared to my vision and the operation was always as I expected."[22] According to Tesla, the principle on which his induction motor operated was as a rotating magnetic field. His machine produced "a sort of magnetic cyclone which grips the rotatable part and whirls it—exactly what my professor had said could never be done."[23]

Above: At Tesla's lab, high tension current passes through Mark Twain's body, lighting Tesla's lamps
Previous: This undated trading card features an illustration of Tesla demonstrating an experiment

Tesla's stamina and productivity was awe inspiring; he "produced as rapidly as the machines could be constructed."[24] In order to gain acceptance in the influential scientific community, Tesla gave one of his two-phase motors to Cornell professor William Anthony not long after opening his laboratory. After a series of tests Anthony proclaimed that "it had an efficiency equal to that of the best direct-current motors" already in use.[25] Tesla was on his way.

Tesla quickly moved to patent his entire alternating-current system. The patent office, however, balked at the idea and insisted that Tesla break the system down into its component parts.[26] In the end, the system comprised seven separate inventions covering "his single and polyphase motors, his distribution system and polyphase transformers."[27] A year later, in 1888, he was granted five more patents covering various versions of the three-phase systems. The next year—eighteen more patents.

This flurry of activity had both positive and negative results. For the negative, Tesla's habit of working superhuman hours without rest

One day Mark Twain dropped by the laboratory and Tesla decided to have a little fun with him. He asked Twain to step up on a small platform and then set the thing vibrating with his oscillator. Twain was thrilled by the gentle sensations running through his body. "This gives you vigor and vitality," he exclaimed. After a short time Tesla warned Twain that he better come down now or risk the consequences. "Not by a jugfull," insisted Twain, "I am enjoying myself." Continuing to extol on the wonderful feeling for several more minutes Twain suddenly stopped talking. Looking pleadingly at Tesla he yelled, "Quick, Tesla! Where is it?" "Right over there," Tesla responded calmly. Off Twain rushed to the restroom, embarrassed by his condition. Tesla smiled; the laxative effect of the vibrator was well known to the chuckling laboratory staff.[34]

was frightening to those around him. He would often work until he collapsed.[28] On the positive side, Tesla's productivity and innovation raised his profile and reputation to extraordinary heights. He was about to enter a new era of his life, one of fame and fortune, and perhaps most surprising to himself, one of climbing the social ladder.

One such social contact was Thomas Commerford Martin. A former seminary student, then Edison employee, then editor of the trade magazine *Electrical World*, Martin persuaded Tesla to write an article for publication and then to present his work to the AIEE. On May 15, 1888, Tesla was invited to deliver his first major lecture on "A New System of Alternating Current Motors and Transformers."[29] O'Neill gives us some insight into the importance of the AIEE lecture:

"This lecture became a classic of the electrical engineering field. In it Tesla presented the theory and practical application of alternating current to power engineering. This, with his patents, described the foundation, in the matter of circuits, machines and operations, and theory, upon which almost the entire electrical system of the country was established and is still operating today. No new development of anything even slightly approaching comparable magnitude has been made in the field of electrical engineering down to the present time."[30]

Following this lecture Martin became somewhat of a publicist for Tesla. In 1893, Martin would publish *The Inventions, Researches, and Writings of Nikola Tesla*, a 500-page opus compiling the publications and lectures of "the greatest living electrician."[31] He would also introduce Tesla to Robert Underwood Johnson, an influential editor of *The Century Magazine*, and his beautiful wife, Katharine. Both Robert and Katharine were enchanted by the charismatic Tesla, whose European intellectuality and flair for reciting poetry in many languages from memory made him the ultimate party guest. As the saying goes, this was the beginning of a beautiful friendship[32] and Tesla enjoyed many delightful evenings at dinner parties thrown at the Johnsons' fine Lexington Avenue brown-stone. Among the "wide range of famous and lively luminaries" that adorned the Johnson's home were the writer Samuel Langhorne Clemens (better known as Mark Twain), naturalist John Muir, and various musicians, actors, and actresses that routinely graced the New York stages.[33] For his part, Tesla would regale the others with recitations of both poetry and his inventions, and commonly the evening would end with Mark Twain, Rudyard Kipling, Anton Dvořák or other guests following Tesla back to his laboratory to witness firsthand some of his electrical marvels.

For someone largely reclusive later in life, Tesla enjoyed a period of being a veritable "social darling, a sought-after guest swirling through Manhattan's most glittering homes, private salons, and lavish restaurants." Tesla himself hosted "elaborate dinner parties in private rooms at the delectable Delmonico's."[35] He would often meet with famous friends at The Players, an exclusive club founded by the famous Shakespearean actor Edwin Booth, older brother of the infamous John Wilkes Booth, who had assassinated Abraham Lincoln many years before. Tesla was enjoying the newfound fame, and the public was eager to hear about his latest inventions. Following another Tesla lecture on "high frequency phenomena" in 1891, along with a glowing article by journalist Joseph

Above: Robert Underwood Johnson, one of Tesla's closest friends

Wetzler in *Harpers Weekly*,[36] Thomas Commerford Martin profiled Tesla in 1894 with the most effusive adulation, noting in *The Century Magazine*:

"Mr. Tesla has been held a visionary, deceived by the flash of casual shooting stars; but the growing conviction of his professional brethren is that because he saw farther he saw first the low lights flickering on tangible new continents of science."[37]

All of this publicity set Tesla up as the genius "that invented the 20th Century,"[38] but Tesla was not very good at commercializing his inventions. He felt that the natural course would be to set up his own company to manufacture his new dynamos, motors, and transformers. But such an enterprise "would take him away from the original experimental work which greatly fascinated him, and which he did not wish to interrupt."[39] Tesla felt that "commercializing his inventions… was a problem that could be postponed."[40] This focus on experiment and innovation, while disregarding commercialization, goes a long way to explaining why Tesla often felt cheated by business partners— and why he ended up destitute at the end of his life.

And then there was George Westinghouse. No matter what you think about his inventive genius, Nikola Tesla would likely have never made any money at all if it had not been for George Westinghouse. Like Edison, Westinghouse was already an accomplished inventor and busi-nessman when Tesla came to New York. A few months older than Edison and ten years Tesla's senior, Westinghouse had made his name and fortune first by inventing a new air brake that became the standard on trains, then with numerous other electrical devices. Also, like Edison, Westinghouse knew how to market his own inventions. But whereas Edison often disdained the ideas of others, Westinghouse was quick to recognize the value of the inventions created by other inventors. Which is how he first came to hear about Tesla.

Opposite: George Westinghouse, ca. 1900–1914

While Edison was committed to the direct current system that used the incandescent bulbs he invented, Westinghouse was open to the idea of alternating current. He had already bought the rights to alternating current patents by the French/English team of Gaulard and Gibbs. But the Gaulard-Gibbs system "still had serious problems."[41] Two years before Tesla's 1888 AIEE lecture, Westinghouse had founded a company to develop "apparatuses for the production, the transmission and the use of alternating current electricity."[42] So a month after the lecture, Westinghouse contacted Tesla to discuss the possibility of licensing his patents.

Westinghouse already had much of what he needed, with William Stanley and Oliver Shallenberger hard at work developing the needed dynamos. But he was "absolutely sure that Tesla's inventions provided all the missing components for the completion of his [alternating current] system."[43] After some tough bargaining by Brown and Peck, Tesla's partners and investors, Westinghouse agreed to pay $20,000 in cash and $50,000 in Westinghouse stock, plus $2.50 royalty per horsepower on every Tesla motor, with a $5,000 minimum paid in royalties the first year, $10,000 the second, and $15,000 the third.[44] Westinghouse felt that "the price to be paid seems rather high" but "if it is the only practicable method for operating a motor by the alternating current" then it was worth the price. Besides, Westinghouse said, he could pass the cost on to the users.[45]

Purchasing the Tesla system, however, was not the end of the process. There still remained the sticky fact that Tesla's motor was designed to work at sixty hertz (sixty oscillations per second) whereas Westinghouse's system required the much higher 133 hertz. So Tesla was off to Pittsburgh to work with Westinghouse's staff in an effort to adapt his motor to the needs of Westinghouse. It was an effort that eventually proved fruitless. Later, it was Westinghouse who adapted to Tesla and the sixty hertz that is the standard today. Frustrated after a year of work in Pittsburgh, Tesla returned to New York, spent some time in Europe lecturing and visiting his family, then back to a new laboratory at 33–35 South Fifth Avenue (now West Broadway). Adapting the motor had been unsuccessful (for now), but the association with Westinghouse was just about to take a major step forward that would immerse them both in a battle with Edison and his direct current, as well as showcase the extra-ordinary advantages of alternating current. Westinghouse and Tesla were going to the World's Fair—The World's Columbian Exposition, to be exact.

Chicago World's Fair

Organizers had been planning a wondrous World's Fair for Chicago's lakefront for many years. One of the centerpieces was the electrification of the main site with many thousands of lightbulbs glistening in the night air. The Columbian Exposition was so named because the fair was a celebration of the four-hundredth anniversary of the discovery of America by Christopher Columbus, although it was intentionally delayed by a year because of the presidential election of 1892 that gave Grover Cleveland a second, though nonconsecutive, term in the White House.[46]

The bidding for the grand showcase—92,000 outdoor incandescent lamps that would light the main grounds for six months—was heated.[47] Charles Coffin, co-founder of the newly formed General Electric Company (a result of the merger of Edison Electric and the Thomson-Houston Electric Company), tried to take advantage of his self-assumed monopoly but was repulsed by the fair's organizers. After a bidding war that pitted Edison's direct current system against Tesla's alternating current system, which was offered by the Westinghouse Company, it was Westinghouse that walked away with the contract.

And what a lucrative contract it turned out to be, although not so much for the selling price, because that was bartered down to what was clearly a bargain for the organizers. Rather, Westinghouse knew that this would be a glorious showcase for Tesla's alternating current system and that success here could mean the beginning of riches for both Tesla and Westinghouse in the future. The Columbian Exposition became "the first public application of Tesla's polyphase alternating-current system."[48] Edison, unhappy at not having received the lighting contract, refused to give Westinghouse a license to produce Edison's patented lightbulb design, the standard in the industry. This necessitated a mad scramble by Westinghouse and his engineers to produce 250,000 modified Sawyer-Man "stopper lamps" as an inferior, but sufficient, substitute.[49]

At almost seven hundred acres, the fair displayed the wares of about sixty thousand exhibitors and over the course of six months welcomed more than twenty-seven million visitors, each paying fifty cents for entry.[50] The site was largely designed by Daniel Burnham and Frederick Law Olmstead, the latter of whom had already designed New York City's Central Park and would go on to design the reservation at Niagara Falls, New York. Displays included Tesla's spinning Egg of Columbus,

Opposite: Exposition grounds, World's Columbian Exposition, Chicago
Following: Electrical Building, World's Columbian Exposition

DEPARTMENT OF ELECTRICITY

FACE FRANKLIN

examples of his alternating-current motors, armatures and generators, and phosphorescent signs in which the names of noted electricians and his favorite Serbian poet were made to glow in the dark.[51] Even more eye-catching was his daring feat of passing one million volts of electricity through his body to the amazement of all. Thomas Edison also had a display highlighting some of his most amazing inventions, including his phonograph, a multichannel telegraph, and a kinetoscope, Edison's early film projector.

Towering over the Court of Honor was the magnificent statue of The Republic, Daniel Chester French's sixty-five-foot-tall gold-gilded plaster behemoth depicting a general (Columbus) overseeing the fair.[52] Not to be outdone, General Electric erected an eighty-two-foot-tall Tower of Light in the center of Electricity Hall.[53] Without a doubt the fair was a marvelous success, with the most impressive display being when the thousands of lights were turned on. As anxious Westinghouse engineers waited, President Cleveland pressed a gold-and-ivory telegraph key and the 2,000-horsepower generators roared

Above: Exposition grounds, World's Columbian Exposition, Chicago

to life. The white stucco Exposition buildings lit up the night as they reflected the never-before-seen electrical light display. As the "White City" erupted into light, Westinghouse and Tesla knew that alternating current would be the electricity of the future.

Above: Tesla's polyphase alternating-current generator, World's Columbian Exposition, Chicago

Niagara Falls

In his autobiography, Tesla reminisces about the first time he heard of Niagara Falls. It was in the schoolroom of the Normal School during his youth. Here "there were a few mechanical models which interested me and turned my attention to water turbines." After hearing a description of the great Niagara Falls, Tesla "pictured in my imagination a big wheel run by the Falls." He proclaimed to his uncle that one day he would "go to America and carry out this scheme."[54]

Tesla now had that opportunity. After their successful collaboration in Chicago, Westinghouse set his sights on using the Tesla system to harness Niagara Falls for electricity generation. Up to this point the only use of the falls had been to build small canals to provide hydropower for mills and a tannery. But many saw the opportunity of channeling the awesome power of the falls to generate electricity.

SCIENTIFIC AMERICAN

[Entered at the Post Office of New York, N. Y., as Second Class matter.   Copyright, 1896, by Munn & Co.]

A WEEKLY JOURNAL OF PRACTICAL INFORMATION, ART, SCIENCE, MECHANICS, CHEMISTRY, AND MANUFACTURES.

Vol. LXXIV.—No. 4.]
Established 1845.

NEW YORK, JANUARY 25, 1896.

[$3.00 A YEAR.
Weekly.

THE POWER CANAL AND BUILDINGS.

INTERIOR OF THE CABLE BRIDGE.

OILING AND COOLING PIPES.   THE DYNAMOS.   THE FRICTION BRAKE.

THE NIAGARA FALLS POWER PLANT.—[See page 55.]

A former Edison board member, Edward Dean Adams, was picked to lead the newly formed Cataract Construction Company and determine the best way to obtain and then distribute electricity from the falls. Despite Thomas Edison's assertions that he could transmit electricity as far as Buffalo, direct current systems were limited to running the machinery of local mills and lighting up some of the local village streets. The limitations of direct current were far too restrictive for any significant distribution.[55]

Tesla's alternating current system was just the answer the Cataract Construction Company was looking for, although they did not know that in the beginning. Adams first headed off to Europe where others were working to exploit alternating current for lighting and power generation. Eventually the Cataract Construction Company offered a contest of sorts, with cash prizes totaling $20,000 for the best plan for harnessing the falls.[56] With more than a few parties claiming the rights to various parts of the alternating current system, there was backstabbing and counter claims and more than a little industrial theft of ideas. But in the end it was Tesla's patents that won the day. The Westinghouse Company was chosen to provide the powerhouse and alternating current system, while the General Electric Company was awarded construction of the transmission lines.

Westinghouse, relying on a dozen Tesla patents, completed the powerhouse in 1895. Its enormous polyphase generator could produce an unprecedented 15,000 horsepower. Within the next year General Electric completed the transmission and distribution system and sufficient electricity to power industries "through the Falls and Buffalo areas."[57] Westinghouse went on to add another seven generating units, raising the power output to 50,000 horsepower. Tesla's patented alternating current system was to change the lives of all Americans as the Niagara project showed investors that alternating current could transmit power over long distances.

Disaster Strikes

This great news was bittersweet for Nikola Tesla. On March 13, 1895, while the Niagara generators using his technology were just about to become operational, Tesla's South Fifth Avenue laboratory burned to the ground, along with all of his equipment, his experiments, his notebooks, and his dreams. The timing was terrible—he had been on the verge of making the "first distance demonstration of his wireless system" (i.e., radio). It was a catastrophe that would lead to yet another conflict about which Tesla would go to war.[58]

Below: Mark Twain and Joseph Jefferson at Tesla's South Fifth Avenue laboratory, New York, 1894

TESLA LABORATORY
LONG ISLAND N.Y.

N. TESLA.
ELECTRO MAGNETIC MOTOR.

No. 381,968.   Patented May 1, 1888.

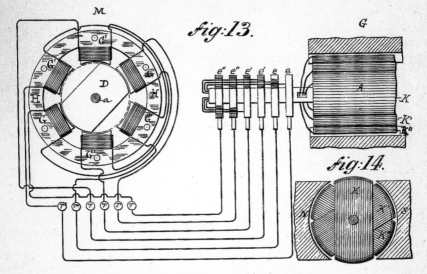

Fig: 13.

Fig: 14.

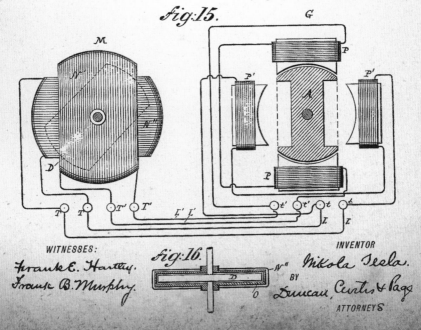

Fig: 15.

Fig: 16.

WITNESSES: INVENTOR

Frank E. Hartley.   Nikola Tesla.
Frank B. Murphy.   BY
                                        Duncan, Curtis & Page
                                                   ATTORNEYS

A MAN ALWAYS AT WAR

When it came to the still infant electricity industry in the late 1800s, Thomas Edison was the man. He had quickly made a name for himself with his inventions and his improvements of the inventions of others. Edison would become one of the most prolific inventors in all history, with more than one thousand U.S. patents to his name, and additional patents in several other countries.[1] His Menlo Park research laboratory was the first of its kind—a veritable invention factory. With teams of scientists and electricians working for him, it was no surprise that he produced hundreds of significant innovations including stock tickers, phonographs, and the precursors to modern-day film-projection systems.

On top of all these individual inventions, Edison had built a fortune developing and distributing electric light and power using the direct current system. Nikola Tesla, like many others, had tried to get Edison interested in alternating current when he was under his employ. But Edison had shown no interest, and after feeling ridiculed and cheated, Tesla had abruptly quit. Later when Tesla teamed up with Edison's archrival George Westinghouse and then went on to beat out Edison for contracts at the Chicago World's Fair and Niagara Falls, Edison was understandably livid. The war of the electric currents had begun.

War of the Electric Currents

While technically Edison did not "invent" the incandescent light—which had seen various developments over nearly three-quarters of century—he did perfect the long-lasting filament that allowed practical use of the lightbulb in industry and homes. More importantly, Edison had also pioneered the commercialization of direct current for transmission of electricity. In part because of the critical nature of this investment in building his wealth, and in part because he truly believed direct current was safer, he was dead set against the development of alternating current. But even Edison understood that direct current had a significant limitation—it could only be transmitted for short distances. This necessitated a direct current power plant every mile or so.

Meanwhile, in early 1888, Westinghouse engineers had developed a meter that solved one of the two key problems holding back commercialization of a rival alternating current system. The meter allowed the current to be more efficiently sold to the user, but it did not solve the main problem of how to turn alternating current into power. Only two months later, however, Nikola Tesla received five patents for his alternating current motor. Some development would still be needed before the Westinghouse machinery and the Tesla alternating current motor

Above: Tesla alternating current motor
Opposite: Thomas Edison, 1925

could be made compatible, but Tesla's motor was a critical step in the shift from direct to alternating current.[2] Tesla had also invented an alternating current transformer that could step up the current to high voltages, which increased the ability to send the current for much longer distances.

Around this same time, English engineer Charles Parson was inventing a steam turbine "that could produce electricity far more efficiently than traditional piston-fired steam engines."[3] The combined innovation of these complementary breakthroughs set the stage for both higher efficiency in producing electricity and the ability to transmit it for long distances, something that could not be done with Edison's direct current systems.

Edison's reaction to the successes of Westinghouse and Tesla was immediate. He had pamphlets printed and mailed to reporters and lighting utilities that were considering purchase of equipment from Edison's rivals. The pamphlets accused Westinghouse and other Edison competitors of being in violation of his patents and warned that anyone buying from them would find themselves without a supplier once the patent infringement cases were settled.[4] Edison also started pushing the idea of the dangers of alternating current at high voltages versus the safety of his low-voltage direct current.

Countering Edison's claims, the proponents of alternating current argued that it was perfectly safe. Raging debates began to occur regularly in various electrical societies like the AIEE, where Tesla had already given several lectures. The journal *Electrician* reported "it is no longer a question of discussing the pros and cons in amicable conclave," but of "fighting tooth and nail."[5]

The technical battle was mostly the dry stuff of scientists, argued deep inside the technical journals and scientific meetings. Like hot-rod aficionados with their engine specifications, electricians argued over the efficiency, reliability, and versatility of the two systems.[6] Most of this was not visible, and certainly not understandable, to the general public. But one thing that was understandable was the occasional death by electrocution. With cities like New York strung tight with hundreds of electrical wires from a dozen electric light utilities, the public feared the occasional might become the frequent.[7]

Edison saw the competition as a personal affront and fought back assertively, even arrogantly. He felt that his oddly quiet former employee and chief professional rival were pushing what Edison considered to be dangerous alternating current onto society. Dangerous in that it ran at higher voltage, but also because it was cutting into his business model based entirely on direct current. To counteract this, Edison made sure the public and those making lighting decisions knew just how dangerous alternating current could be. His ultimate goal was to get the state to ban the use of alternating current as unsafe, thus giving his direct current systems the ability to expand unhindered by this new competition.

Accidental Death by Electrocution

Edison got some help in this regard from a few grizzly electrocutions that occurred over a short period of time. One such occasion was the unfortunate circumstance of an electrical repairman named John Feeks. Back in the late 1800s the streets of New York City had quickly become a morass of hundreds of naked exposed electric wires stretched from masts that looked like trees spreading their branches in even rows. Feeks and others would climb the poles and cut through old wires to replace them with new wires. Sometimes the dead wires were not so dead. On October 11, 1889, Feeks accidentally touched a live wire, which not only sent a jolt of high-voltage electricity coursing through his body but dislodged him from his perch and sent him crashing into a spider's web of charged wires stretched below. There he dangled for more than forty-five minutes. Horrified pedestrians on the street below were unlucky enough to see streaks of light flashing from Feeks' mouth, feet, hands, and nose. Such a gruesome scene bolstered Edison's case that alternating current was too dangerous to be used while direct current—on which his own systems were based—was safe.[8]

A few accidents, however, were not going to be enough to convince the public that alternating current should be banned from all use. It would take a lot more death to do that.

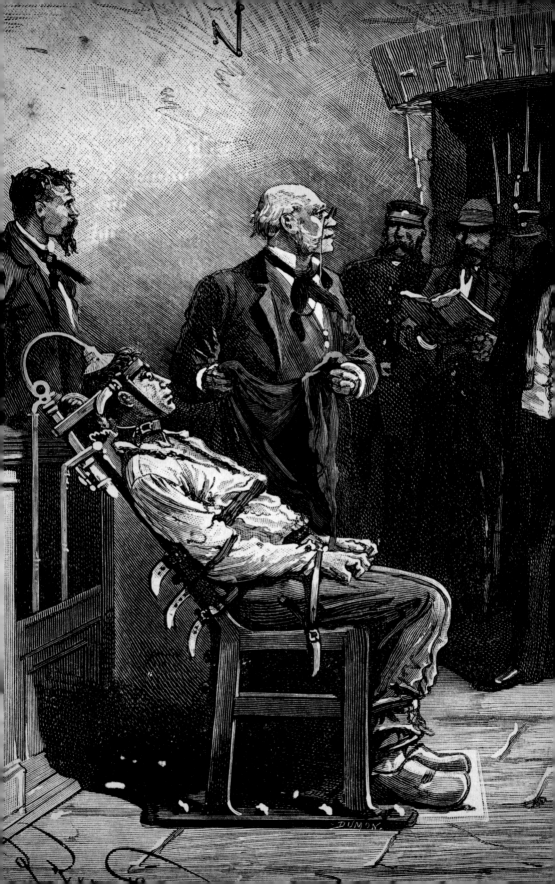

Intentional Death by Electrocution

Ever the opportunist, Edison enlisted the help of Harold Pitney Brown, an electrician with a decade of experience and a bit of a mean streak. Not long before, in an 1885 speech, New York Governor David B. Hill had opined that the "present mode of executing criminals by hanging has come down to us from the dark ages."[9] He was looking for an alternative. Meanwhile, Edison had actively lobbied to replace the usual methods of execution (morphine or hanging) with electricity, proposing to use alternating current because of the high voltages achievable in the transmission wires.

Alfred Porter Southwick was a dentist and a believer in the death penalty for egregious crimes. When Southwick heard about Governor Hill's desire to remove the cause of objections to capital punishment, i.e., the sheer gruesomeness of the deed, Southwick was ready with his solution. After all, he had been capturing stray dogs for years and killing them with electricity, so he knew that it would work. Southwick used his political connections to get a commission created to evaluate more humane alternatives, and then got appointed as one of the three guiding members. After extensive research, and many deaths of stray dogs, the commission, which had intended to declare electricity as the answer from the beginning, had reached a surprising impasse. One of the members, Elbridge Gerry, a highly respected high-society member who also served as legal counsel to the American Society for the Prevention of Cruelty to Animals,[10] was leaning toward morphine injection as the most humane method.

Then Thomas Edison wrote him a letter. The sheer weight of Edison's reputation was enough to convince Gerry. "I certainly had no doubt after hearing his statement," he would later say.[11] The commission made their recommendation, a bill was passed, and on June 4, 1888, Governor Hill signed the bill into law.

One day later Harold Pitney Brown had a letter printed in the *New York Evening Post* that called for the ban of alternating current high-voltage overhead lines. Perhaps not knowing how right he was

Opposite: William Kemmler, the first man to be electrocuted by electric chair, August 6, 1890

under certain circumstances, he pronounced that the "damnable" alternating current was dangerous to human life.[12] "The public must submit to constant danger from sudden death," Brown wrote, "in order that a corporation may pay a little larger dividend."

Proponents of alternating current, including George Westinghouse, argued that the seemingly independent Brown was actually in cahoots with Thomas Edison, a charge that Brown denied. As the questions of which was more dangerous grew, Brown claimed he "called upon Mr. Thos. A. Edison, whom I had never before met" and to his surprise "Mr. Edison at once invited me to make the experiments at his private laboratory.[13] This seemed conveniently suspicious to both Westinghouse and the local press. The *New York Sun* ran an exposé on Brown and found that he had been paid by both the Edison Company and the Thomson-Houston company, the primary purpose being to injure the reputation of their mutual rival—Westinghouse.[14]

In any case, Brown went to work paying local neighborhood boys twenty-five cents apiece for "stray" dogs, which he duly electrocuted. Many poor dogs and a few letters later it was clear that Edison had nearly convinced the state legislators in New York that alternating current was much too dangerous to use for public distribution of electricity. Later, Edison even staged the electrocution of Topsy, a female elephant at the Luna Park Zoo at Coney Island, whose poor temperament and big feet had led to the deaths of three handlers in three years. The brutal electrocution was filmed and showed just how deadly alternating current could be, even to something quite a bit larger than an average human being.[15]

Edison called these animal executions getting "Westinghoused" because of the use of the alternating current system that his main competitor, using Tesla's technology, was developing.[16] Later the term "Westinghoused" would be applied to the first execution by electrical current.[17] On August 6, 1890, New York State accomplished the first execution using the new alternating-current electric chair. William Kemmler had murdered his philandering wife with an axe and then calmly asked his son to contact the local police. He was tried, found guilty, and sentenced to death. Edison had convinced the board that

Previous: An illustration of the oscillator's capacity for producing electrical explosions of great power

Kemmler's death would be rapid and painless because of the incredibly high voltages by the dangerous alternating current.

When the day came, however, the execution did not go smoothly. An initial surge of more than one thousand volts of electricity was applied to Kemmler for seventeen seconds as he sat in the newly designed electric chair. This seemed to work and he was pronounced dead by the attending doctor. Suddenly Kemmler's chest heaved and a droning rasp grew from his foaming lips. He emitted an animal-like cry and his body began shaking violently. Desperately, the attendants raced to reattach the electrodes to his skull and body and then switched the dynamo back onto full power. Wanting to ensure that they did not have a repeat of the failed first attempt, for nearly two more minutes the electricity surged into Kemmler as "the stench of burning flesh filled the room."[18]

Despite these gruesome incidents and Edison's public relations attempts to discredit alternating current, the winner of the war of the electric currents was clearly the alternating current commercialized by Westinghouse that relied on Tesla's many patents. Alternating current would go on to replace direct current for almost all generation and distribution of electricity to industry and households. Edison would, of course, go on to develop hundreds of new inventions and improvements right up until his death in 1931 at the age of eighty-four, but this war—the war of the currents—was won by George Westinghouse and Nikola Tesla.

Above: Topsy the elephant, electrocuted by Thomas Edison in Coney Island's Luna Park, 1903

War of the Radio

"Mr. Marconi is a donkey."[18]

This uncharacteristic bluntness from the usually polite Tesla is a good indication of his feelings toward Guglielmo Marconi. Tesla had reason to hold Marconi in such contempt, as the Italian inventor had become world renowned in large part by borrowing Tesla's ideas and apparatuses in the invention of wireless telegraphy, what we now call radio.

The reality of the invention of radio, like most inventions, is much more complex. Tesla had begun his research into "wireless" as far back as 1891. A year later, in lectures delivered in London and Paris, Tesla for the first time suggested that messages could be transmitted wirelessly.[20] Over the next few years he investigated the transmission of electromagnetic energy without wires, ostensibly building the first radio transmitter.[21] In 1893 he demonstrated his wireless communication ideas by delivering a lecture in St. Louis called "On Light and Other High Frequency Phenomena," and then not long afterward also addressed the Franklin Institute and National Electric Light Association, both in Philadelphia. Certainly many others had contributed knowledge to the development of radio transmissions, both before and after Tesla. But Tesla provided some of the more fundamental principles and patents and his work was widely publicized.[22]

Then came the disaster of 1895, when his South Fifth Avenue laboratory burned down, destroying all his work. Radio, at least for Tesla, would take a back seat while he reestablished his laboratory capabilities. Tesla also would be distracted with other projects, and move on to Colorado to do additional research to perfect his wireless energy principles. But while he was otherwise preoccupied Marconi was busy developing wireless communication. The Italian, who had read about Tesla's work, began working

Opposite: Guglielmo Marconi

on modifications to earlier apparatuses in an effort to create transmitters and receivers. By the end of 1895 Marconi had transmitted radio signals for about one mile, a significant achievement. The next year he went public with his device. Right away those in the know felt that it resembled Tesla's devices, demonstrations, and patents, something that Marconi denied. A year later Marconi received a British patent for a radio transmission and receiving system.[23] Marconi had invented radio. Sort of.

At first Tesla had little to say about Marconi's apparent expropriation of his own hard-earned discoveries. But clearly there was animosity building. Tesla would demonstrate radio-controlled boats in Madison Square Garden and work on wireless telegraphy in Colorado Springs and then Wardenclyffe, his wireless transmission laboratory on Long Island, but these efforts would be overshadowed by Marconi's "successful" transmission of the letter "S" (dot–dot–dot) from Poldhu, Cornwall, England to Signal Hill, St. John's, Newfoundland.[24]

Worse, Marconi was awarded the Nobel Prize for Physics in 1909—for invention of the radio. By 1915 Tesla had had enough and filed a lawsuit against Marconi for infringing on his patents. Tesla's goal was to obtain a court injunction against Marconi's claim to have invented radio.

Above: This U.S. Navy shipboard transmitter was manufactured using six of Tesla's patents
Opposite: Tesla Radio advertising poster

Unfortunately the lawsuit failed and Marconi's work was still considered to have been the precursor for the invention.

Those believing in fate may find the irony in the events of three decades later. Marconi, feeling that the federal government was infringing on his, that is, Marconi's patents for radio, sued the government. The case went all the way to the Supreme Court, who after due deliberations reached their decision. Not only did the federal government not infringe on Marconi's patents, they said, but Marconi had actually infringed on the patents of Tesla. Tesla's original patent (No. 645576) was reinstated as predecessor—Tesla, not Marconi, had invented the radio. Unfortunately the Supreme Court decision came several months after Tesla had passed away penniless in his sleep.

War of Finances

Battling over whether direct or alternating current would win the day or who invented radio would not be the only battles fought by Tesla. A much more ingrained war that Tesla fought his entire life was the war over finances. And usually, he was losing.

Early on Tesla was prone to feel cheated by his employers, first by Edison's men in Paris and then by Edison himself in New York.

Tesla also felt cheated by his investors when he first set up the Tesla Electric Light and Manufacturing Company. Even when he did not feel he was being used Tesla struggled to obtain the funds he needed for his research. And that research was expensive. In the late 1800s one could not apply for government grants to do basic research as is the case in modern times. Most funding came from private investors such as J. Pierpont Morgan and John Jacob Astor, both of whom were investing in Edison and Westinghouse's operations as well as Tesla's. Morgan's house, in fact, was the first to be lit up with Edison's direct current. Overall, money was always tight and Tesla often begged profusely for more funding.

The need for funding encompassed not just his expensive and sometimes speculative research in electricity. Tesla was also someone who liked to live richly—even when his finances would prudently suggest a more austere lifestyle. Tesla frequented the upscale Delmonico's restaurant in New York, usually dining alone but sometimes with some of the restaurant's other famous patrons like Mark Twain and Robert Underwood Johnson. Delmonico's was also graced by such personalities as Jenny Lind, Theodore Roosevelt, Diamond Jim Brady, Charles Dickens, Oscar Wilde and even Napoleon III of France. The food was wonderful, but it did not come cheaply.[25]

Tesla's expenses also included the kid leather gloves, European-made shoes with spats, and other finely tailored clothing that he preferred to wear, much of which he disposed of after only a week or two because of his aversion to germs. He lived in expensive hotels and

Above: John Jacob Astor IV, 1909

had most meals in the hotel restaurants. All of these exorbitant expenses increased his cost of living immeasurably beyond the usual costs of running a laboratory with several assistants on the payroll.

One financial decision would come to haunt him throughout his life, but especially in his later years. His initial contract with George Westinghouse included a rather lucrative patent purchase price plus a royalty for each horsepower produced. The dire financial strain of the late 1890s had impacted both Westinghouse and Edison to the point where Westinghouse asked Tesla to remove the royalty fee for a set buy-out of his patents. Feeling that his inventions would change the world, and not being a particularly good manager of money, Tesla agreed. The decision likely cost him many millions of dollars over the rest of his lifetime.[26]

Eventually all of his patrons would stop funding him and Tesla became financially destitute. Ironically, thankful for all the financing he did receive over the years, it was Tesla who defended J.P. Morgan when others accused the wealthy financier of pulling funding because

Tesla's wireless electrical power ideas would not provide a profit for Morgan. In his autobiography, Tesla noted with respect to Morgan that "he carried out his generous promise to the letter and it would have been most unreasonable to expect from him anything more." It was not lack of faith in his abilities by Morgan that would end Tesla's work at Wardenclyffe, it was that "my project was retarded by laws of nature. The world was not prepared for it. It was too far ahead of time. But the same laws will prevail in the end and make it a triumphal success."[27]

Opposite: J. Pierpont Morgan, 1902

In the end, Tesla would be completely broke. He would receive a small stipend from the Yugoslavian government to help with basic living expenses and the Westinghouse Company would pick up the New Yorker Hotel tab for his meager existence over the last decade of his life.

But that would be later. For now, Wardenclyffe was still a vision in Tesla's eye. He was about to embark on his journey to create wireless communication and energy.

Below: Tesla oscillator as pictured in *The Century Magazine*, 1895

TESLA LABORATORY
LONG ISLAND N.Y.

No. 645,576.

N. TESLA.

Patented Mar. 20, 1900.

SYSTEM OF TRANSMISSION OF ELECTRICAL ENERGY.

(Application filed Sept. 2, 1897.)

(No Model.)

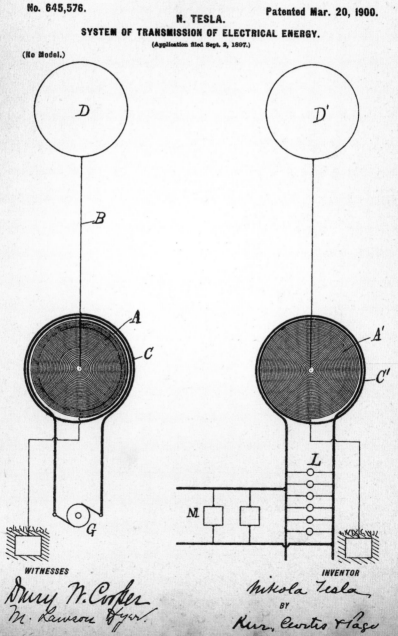

WITNESSES

Drury W. Cooper

M. Lawson Dyer

INVENTOR

Nikola Tesla

BY

Kerr, Curtis & Page

ATTORNEYS.

WIRELESS AND WARDENCLYFFE

Aﬀter Tesla returned from his consultant job with Westinghouse in Pittsburgh and resumed work in his new laboratory in New York City, he "experienced one of the greatest moments" of his life—the first demonstration of wireless light.[1] Not one to restrain his hyperbole, Tesla recalls that "it was in November, 1890, that I performed a laboratory experiment which was one of the most extraordinary and spectacular ever recorded in the annals of science."[2] He had satisfied himself that a high frequency electric field of sufficient intensity could be produced to light up vacuum tubes, and built a transformer to test his theory.

Late one night Tesla took a position in the center of the laboratory, with no connection to the machine being tested. Picking up a long glass tube in each hand Tesla instructed his assistants to throw the switch. In a display that could have inspired Luke Skywalker's lightsaber duels eight decades later, the tubes instantly became "brilliant swords of fire."[3]

The immediate impact on his assistants, according to Tesla, was fear of "so new and wonderful [a] spectacle." They thought he was a magician or hypnotist. But using Tesla's discoveries, wireless light had become a reality.[4]

Impressing his laboratory staff and some hoity-toity electrical engineering societies, however, was not nearly enough to pay the bills. Tesla had to go public. The first real public demonstration of the wireless lighting took place during the Columbian Exposition in Chicago in 1893. Playing the showman, Tesla lit a gas-discharge lamp wirelessly using high-voltage, high-frequency alternating current. Just as he had done in London two years earlier, Tesla held up the lamp bulbs in his hands and they glowed magnificently. All without any wires connecting them to the transformers.[5] According to witnesses, the marvelous demonstrations had "produced so much wonder and astonishment" that the crowd bubbled in amazement.[6]

Later Tesla devoted himself to the wireless transmission not just of light, but of power. In 1921 he would predict that "power can be, and at no distant date will be, transmitted without wires, for all commercial uses, such as the lighting of homes and the driving of aeroplanes."[7] Tesla also understood that "it only remains to develop them commercially," something that was not his strong suit.

"I am firmly convinced that it can be done, and I hope that we shall live to see it done."

—Tesla, lecture to National Electric Light Association, Philadelphia, 1893

Tesla believed that he had the matter of transmitting power wirelessly so well in hand that he claimed he was ready to transmit 100,000 horsepower by wireless with only minor losses of energy. This, he believed, could be done "whether the distance was one mile or ten thousand miles, and the power can be collected high in the air, underground, or on the ground."[8] Still, bringing this idea to fruition would not be easy.

Opposite: Tesla holding a gas-filled phosphor-coated wireless lightbulb that he developed in the 1890s—half a century before fluorescent lamps came into use

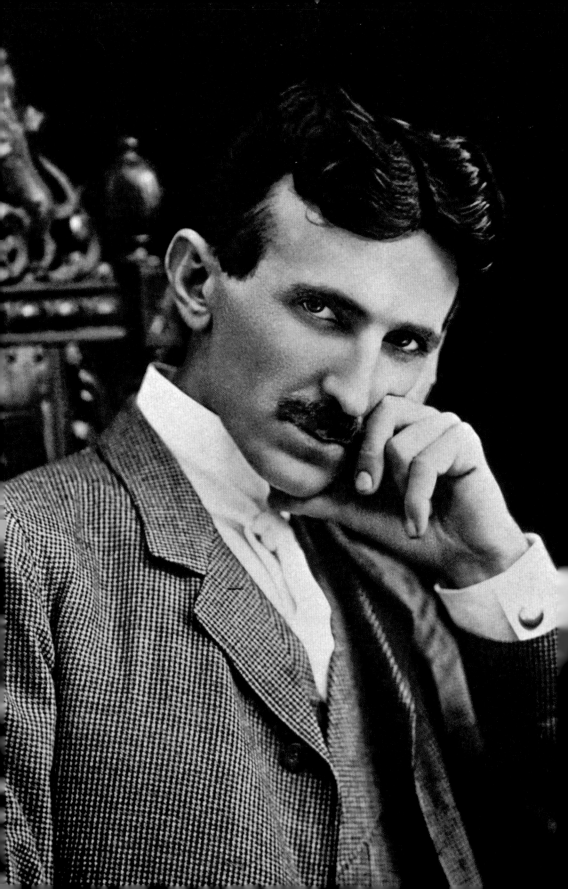

As he struggled to find just the right technology, Tesla tried various configurations of his coiled transformer. Initially he worked with spheres, but he also produced cone-shaped transformers. One conical coil reached one hundred million volts, which he figured was the voltage of a flash of lightning.[9] He knew that he could achieve higher electrical forces with larger apparatuses, but instinctively he felt that he could achieve the same with properly designed smaller transformers. He settled on a flat, spiral coil and with it also achieved the 100 million volt level—"the limit obtainable without risk of accident."[10]

While his Tesla coil research was proceeding, Tesla was also moving forward with his wireless radio experimentation. In "The Art of Telautomatics," Tesla refers to a remote-controlled boat he described in *The Century Magazine* and demonstrated in Madison Square Garden back in 1898.[11] In order to show how wireless technology could be used to command ships and missiles from a distance, Tesla had a large tank built

in the center of the arena in which he placed "an iron-hulled boat a few feet long, shaped like an arc."[12] The audience, mostly attendees of the first annual Electrical Exhibition, was requested to ask questions and the automaton would answer them by signs, usually by turning left or right

Opposite: The dashing Mr. Tesla
Following: The Astor House

or reversing direction. "This was considered magic at the time," writes Tesla, "but was extremely simple, for it was myself who gave the replies by means of the device."[13] He repeated the exercise with a more advanced and larger telautomatic boat in 1919. While Tesla acknowledged that these were "the first and rather crude steps in the evolution of the art of telautomatics," it did signal the beginning of what today we might call robotics. Consider Tesla's designs then and the remote-controlled drones used in our more recent military and terrorist control efforts and you can see how far he was ahead of his time.

All of these achievements were thrilling, but he soon found the space, not to mention safety concerns, were all too limiting in his New York laboratory. So with an invitation from Leonard Curtis and a $30,000 feed stake from Col. John Jacob Astor (owner of the Waldorf-Astoria), Tesla was off to Colorado.[14]

Above: Parts of Tesla's electrical oscillator

Colorado Springs

Colorado Springs offered space and much needed solitude away from the bustling city streets of Manhattan. At over a mile above sea level, Colorado Springs also was one of the most active lightning strike areas in the United States. With promises of unlimited free electric power from the newly built alternating-current distribution system, the city was a natural location for Tesla to continue his wireless research. During his nine-month stay in Colorado, beginning in June 1899 and ending in January 1900, Tesla kept voluminous notes and drawings, explicitly detailing his many experiments.[15] Scientists are still poring through those notes today to see what other wonders may yet to be discovered from Tesla's work.

While in Colorado he made detailed studies of the frequent natural lightning in the area, and used this knowledge as he constructed his apparatuses. Tesla learned so much that he even predicted a lightning strike that nearly destroyed his laboratory before it was even finished. Observing "a heavy cloud over Pikes Peak" and witnessing a lightning strike about ten miles away, Tesla quickly calculated that the shock wave would reach his laboratory in 48.5 seconds.

Above: Tesla in his office demonstrating and electrical apparatus, 1916

GREAT SCIENTIFIC DISCOVERY *Impends*
—Nikola Tesla

"I Positively Expect That Within the Next Decade New Sources of Energy Will Be Opened Up Which Will Put at the Disposal of Mankind Everywhere Power in Unlimited Amounts—I Have Made a Discovery Which I Expect to Announce Soon"

By Harry Goldberg

NIKOLA TESLA, the noted inventor, is preparing to make public within the near future the announcement of a discovery which will make available to the world new sources of energy.

As this discovery will make it possible to tap inexhaustible streams of power at any point on the globe, great changes will follow in social life. Government will become a sort of officious policeman, busybody and benevolent tyrant which will convert the human race into a society like the bees.

What this noted scientist has found is not a form of atomic energy, which he declares to be a fantastic hope, but it is a "universal truth" of such a nature that probably it cannot even be patented. To quote his exact words:

"I positively expect that within the next decade new sources of energy will be opened up which will put at the disposal of mankind everywhere power in unlimited amounts.

"In this connection I have made a discovery which I expect to announce as soon as I have worked out the theory and design of apparatus for practical purposes.

"I want to be emphatic to my concerning the idea that atomic energy will ever be our source of power. This is an illusory idea sacred which I have preached for years. In my experiments with peculiar vacuum tubes operated under tensions of 12,000,000 volts atoms are shattered, but there is no liberation of energy observable such as would be expected according to modern theories. But even if the latter were true, it still would take much more energy to disintegrate the atom than can be recovered by harnessing the liberated energy, however great it might be.

"What I am referring to is an entirely new principle which I have already experimentally demonstrated."

ASKED if his source of energy was electricity, sun power or some other force already known, Dr. Tesla shook his head negatively and refused to affirm any guess, indicating that he would choose a scientific forum from which to make the definite announcement when he was ready.

"Will revolutionary changes follow?"

"I don't believe they will. New ideas are adopted gradually. It is inevitable that those who are in the forefront of the advance will keep their places. Our life is now so regulated that no advance whatever could completely upset the existing order."

[...]

Men Are Like Bees

LEISURE—"Too much leisure, and civilization will go to pot. Man was born to work and suffer and struggle; if he doesn't, he will go under."

MATERIALISM—"Technical advances are inevitably driving us toward the grossest kind of materialism. Before long the social system of bee life will become universal."

LIFE OF PLANETS—"There must be life on other planets. The sun shines. The stars give out heat. Water collects on the surface. Chemical changes occur that we do not yet understand."

—NIKOLA TESLA.

"Exactly with the lapse of this time interval a terrific blow struck the building which might have been thrown off the foundation had it not been strongly braced. All of the windows on one side and a door were demolished and much damage was done to the interior."[16]

Tesla believed that it was possible to transmit electric energy through the earth under the proper conditions of resonance, "thus dispensing with all artificial conductors."[17] But for this to be possible the earth had to be an electrically charged body. Tesla "quickly discovered that the earth is charged to an extremely high potential and is provided with some kind of a mechanism for maintaining its voltage."[18]

"The earth was found to be, literally, alive with electrical vibrations."[19]

Describing what he referred to as "a truth of overwhelming importance for the advancement of humanity," Tesla related how he recorded, in regularly recurring intervals, what he understood to be stationary waves. "Impossible as it seemed," Tesla later wrote, "this planet, despite its vast extent, behaved like a conductor of limited dimensions." Already the significance of this phenomenon as it relates to the transmission of energy had become clear to Tesla. "Not only was it practicable to send telegraphic messages to any distance without wires, as I recognized long ago, but also to impress upon the entire globe the faint modulations of the human voice, far more still, to transmit power, in unlimited amounts, to any terrestrial distance and almost without loss." In fact, he suggested that it was even possible that power could be increased with the distance from the source.[20]

In any case, the main focus of his stay in Colorado was building on his work with wireless transmission that was so ingloriously cut short in

Opposite: *Galveston Daily News*, 1932

the destructive fire of 1895. Tesla began conducting wireless telegraphy experiments with a goal of perfecting the long-range transmission of radio signals. He told local reporters that he would transmit from nearby Pikes Peak to Paris. He made many improvements and refinements to the existing apparatuses, thus enabling him to "generate currents of any tension that may be desired."[21] In some of his experiments he tested the idea of how to "tune" a wireless transmitter to respond to specific signals while rejecting others. This improvement was critical for the development of wireless transmission in order to avoid the interception of a signal by others, a significant concern in the "war to end all wars" (World War I) that would arrive in the not too distant future.[22]

With this knowledge and with his magnifying transmitter—a huge Tesla coil—Tesla was ready to try some large-scale experiments way beyond any scope he could have accomplished in his little New York City laboratory. His longtime assistant, Kolman Czito, had made all the preparations. The primary device was a fencelike wall seventy-five feet in diameter, around which were wound "the turns of the giant primary coil." Inside was a secondary coil "about ten feet in diameter," also wound with wire. In the center of this coil stood a two-hundred-foot-tall mast stretching through the open roof into the crisp Colorado sky, a three-foot copper ball gracing its point.[23]

As instructed by Tesla, Czito closed the switch for exactly one second as Tesla watched the coil from the open doorway. Electrical charges glistened around the secondary coil, then immediately were gone as the switch was again opened. Satisfied that all was working after another short test, Tesla told Czito to close the switch on his command and hold it closed until Tesla told him to open it. Once Tesla got outside where he could watch the copper ball on the tip of the mast, the command was given:

"Czito, close the switch-now!"[24]

Opposite: A loop of wire with current passing through it illustrates the phenomenon of impedance
Following: Burning atmospheric nitrogen with twelve million volts and a sixty-five-foot flame

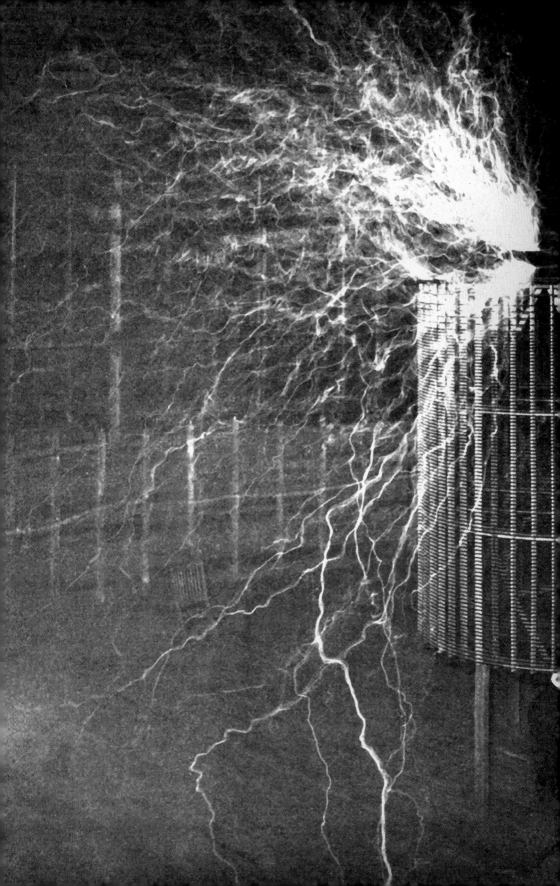

As with the brief contacts, the secondary coil became immersed in electrical fire. But now, with the extended contact the electricity crackled and popped with energy. Soon the crackling turned to sharper snapping like rifle fire, then roared like cannons. "The thunder was terrifying and the thunder shook the building in a most threatening fashion."[25]

Outside, Tesla stood in awe of his own device. Streaks of lightning shot from the ball. First extending only about 10 feet, then twenty feet, then thirty … forty … eighty feet. Finally, bright blue bolts

Above: Spark discharges from a so-called "Tesla coil" at his wireless plant at Colorado Springs, 1899

Above: Tesla's outdoor experiments were sometimes less visually impressive

of lightning more than 135 feet long were shooting out from the ball farther than the width of the building itself. Tesla was even creating thunder. It was the most spectacular sight, even to someone who had been creating electrical charges nearly all his life. Tesla marveled at all that this accomplishment could do for bettering the lives of mankind throughout the world.

And then, nothing. The whole apparatus went dead. No lightning, not even the slightest spark. The entire laboratory was dark.

Furious, Tesla called up the Colorado Springs powerhouse to complain about having his power cut off. Only then did he realize that not only his laboratory, but the entire city, had lost power. Tesla's experiments had knocked the city's generator offline, and worse, it was on fire.

Tesla had overstayed his welcome. The city later charged him for all of the "free electricity" that had been promised when he agreed to move to Colorado. Feeling both elated by his discoveries and dejected by how he was treated, Tesla made plans to return to New York.

Wardenclyffe

Having advanced his wireless transmission of radio waves and energy in Colorado, in early 1900 Tesla returned home to New York with a plan. He envisioned the ability to broadcast under multiple wavelengths from a single station. Receiving 200 acres in a prime location near present day Shoreham, Long Island, and an influx of money from venture capitalists—including a massive $150,000 stake from industrialist J. Pierpont Morgan alone—Tesla began working on the facility and tower that would be named Wardenclyffe.

Designed by famous architect Stanford White, Wardenclyffe consisted of an odd-looking tower about "187 feet high, having a spherical

Above: Colorado Springs Project

terminal about 68 feet in diameter."[26] Tesla insisted that these dimensions were sufficient "for the transmission of virtually any amount of energy."[27] Right from the beginning, however, there were design problems. Many contractors balked at the idea of building such a large skeleton of wood topped by a large semicircular electrode that presented itself like a sail to the wind. Tesla also quickly used up the money provided by Morgan, who was not too pleased about the idea of continuing to finance an operation that may never produce results or provide him any return on his investment.

The new laboratory at Wardenclyffe rose ominously on Long Island's north shore. The tower shadowed the low brick building that housed the dynamos and other experimental machinery. Once all the equipment from the Houston Street laboratory was moved to Wardenclyffe in June 1902, Tesla stopped commuting from the city and rented a nearby cottage for about a year.[28] He continued to do preliminary experiments as construction moved forward, although this occurred unevenly because of financial difficulties and last-minute design changes. Wardenclyffe was much more expensive to build than either Tesla or Morgan had anticipated.

Above: Illustration of Tesla's World Wide Wireless transmission system
Following: The tower at Wardenclyffe

But Wardenclyffe was to be the site where Tesla's World Wireless System would provide a lucrative commercial exploitation of his long-theorized wireless communication system. This world system combined several of Tesla's inventions and made possible "not only the instantaneous and precise wireless transmission of any kind of signals, messages or characters, to all parts of the world, but also the inter-connection of the existing telegraph, telephone, and other signal stations without any change in their present equipment."[29]

The basic principles were relatively simple.[30] The Earth would act as a conductor of electrical energy, much like a current flowing through a wire or other conductors. A grounded Tesla coil transmitter would create a large displacement of the Earth's electric charge. A similar Tesla coil tuned to the same frequency could be used as the receiver, and the energy would flow wirelessly through the Earth from one to the other. Whether this would actually work was something that neither Tesla nor anyone else to date has been able to determine.[31]

The "World Wireless System" is based on the application of the following important inventions and discoveries:[32]

- The "Tesla Transformer" Produces electrical vibrations with currents many times stronger than any ever generated in the usual ways, and sparks more than one hundred feet long.
- The "Magnifying Transmitter" An enhanced transformer specially adapted to transmit electrical energy through the Earth.
- The "Tesla Wireless System" The complete system comprises a number of improvements and is the only means known for transmitting economically electrical energy to a distance without wires.
- The "Art of Individualization" This invention makes possible the transmission of signals or messages absolutely secret and exclusive both in the active and passive aspect, that is, non-interfering as well as non-interferable.
- "The Terrestrial Stationary Waves" The Earth is responsive to electrical vibrations of definite pitch just as a tuning fork to certain waves of sound. These particular electrical vibrations are capable of powerfully exciting the Globe.[32]

Unfortunately, the "Panic of 1901" had severely strained the available investment opportunities for continuing the wireless work. Tesla wrote to J. Pierpont Morgan repeatedly asking for additional funds, all without reply. Then came Marconi's transmission of the letter "S" from England to Newfoundland. Marconi, using ideas patented by Tesla, had beaten Tesla to the punch. Morgan was livid. Tesla was frantic. By mid-1903 the future of Wardenclyffe looked bleak and Tesla wrote Morgan again—this time to impress upon him that his World Wireless System could accomplish much more than just the wireless communication intended for the tower, it could also provide wireless transmission of electric power.[33] Morgan remained unimpressed. Not seeing how he could make any profit from this "free energy," he replied in late 1904 that it would "be impossible for [him] to do anything in the matter." Morgan also discouraged other financiers from investing in Tesla's enterprise. With Tesla's earlier alternating current motor patents, and their associated royalties, expiring in 1905, Tesla was quickly running out of money to fund Wardenclyffe.[34]

Previous: Interior of Wardenclyffe
Opposite: Guglielmo Marconi

U. S. Blows Up

SUSPECTING that German spies were using the big wireless tower erected at Shoreham, L. I., about twenty years ago by Nikola Tesla, the Federal Government ordered the tower destroyed and it was recently demolished with dynamite. During the past month several strangers had been seen lurking about the place.

Tesla erected the tower, which was about 185 feet high, with a well about 100 feet deep, for use in experimenting with the transmission of electrical energy for power and lighting purposes by wireless. The equipment cost nearly $200,-000.

The late J. P. Morgan backed Nikola Tesla with the money to build this remarkable steel tower, that he might experiment in wireless even before people knew of Marconi. A complete description, revised by Dr. Tesla himself, of this unique and ultra-powerful radio plant was given in the March, 1916, issue of THE ELECTRICAL EXPERIMENTER. Everyone interested in the study of high frequency currents should not fail to study that discourse as it contains the theory of how this master electrician proposed to charge this

gone on record as in accordance with derful still is the f

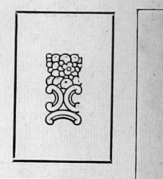

mulgated his basic transmission a grea of his patents and

sla Radio Tower

their belief to be
sla's. More won-
this scientist pro-

some of the water into the pump and force it back into the ball by pushing on the piston handle, this change in pressure will be indicated on the gage secured to the opposite side of the sphere. In this way the Tesla earth currents are supposed to act.

The patents of Dr. Tesla are basically quite different from those of Marconi and others in the wireless telegraphic field. In the nature of things this would be expected to be the case, as Tesla believes and has designed apparatus intended for the *transmission of large amounts of electrical energy,* while the energy received in the transmission of intelligence wirelessly amounts to but a few millionths of an ampere in most cases by the time the current so transmitted has been picked up a thousand miles away. In the Hertzian wave system,

Two Views of the Last Minutes of Tesla's Gigantic Radio Tower at Shoreham, L. I., New York, As It Was Being Demolished by the Federal Government. It Was Suspected That German Spies Were Using the Tower for Radio - Communication Purposes. It Stood 185 Feet Above the Ground and Cost About $200,000. Tesla Had Not Used It For Several Years.
Photos by American Press Association

of *earth current* years ago in some blications. Brief-

as it has been explained and believed in, the energy is transmitted with a very large loss to the receptor by electro-magnetic waves which pass out laterally from the transmit-

While Tesla did accomplish some useful things on the site, including invention of his bladeless turbine and sales of Tesla coils, for all essential purposes the Wardenclyffe experiment was over. Wardenclyffe was eventually transferred to George Boldt of the Waldorf-Astoria in payment for all the years of unpaid hotel charges accrued to Tesla. Depending on who is telling the story, the tower was destroyed in 1917 either by a contractor for scrap so that Boldt could recoup some of his lost income, or by the government to keep it from being used by German spies. The original laboratory building itself remains today after being used as a photographic processing site for many decades.

After Wardenclyffe Tesla did manage to get several radio towers built at Telefunken Wireless, a new company set up in Sayville on the south shore of Long Island. Telefunken served as the American connection for a North America-Europe wireless communication network. But by this time Tesla was merely assisting in the design and building of a series of radio towers. Tesla was not finished inventing, but the most productive time of his life was slowly coming to an end.

TESLA LABORATORY
LONG ISLAND N.Y.

No. 685,956.

N. TESLA.

Patented Nov. 5, 1901.

APPARATUS FOR UTILIZING EFFECTS TRANSMITTED THROUGH NATURAL MEDIA.

(Application filed Nov. 2, 1899. Renewed May 29, 1901.)

(No Model.)

Fig. 1

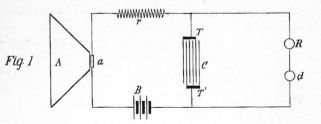

Fig. 2

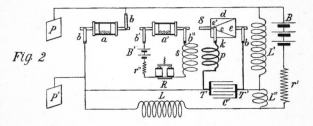

Fig. 3

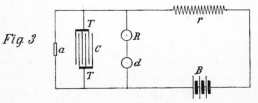

Fig. 4

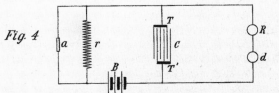

Fig. 5

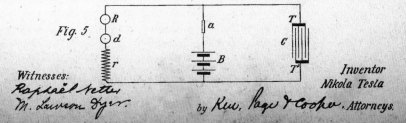

Witnesses:
Raphaël Netter
M. Lawson Dyer.

Inventor
Nikola Tesla
by Kerr, Page & Cooper. Attorneys.

TAKING ON EINSTEIN

Rotating magnetic fields, alternating current motors and transformers, the Tesla coil, wireless transmission of radio communication, wireless lighting . . . Nikola Tesla had no shortage of inventions that he could call his own. But these were not the only inventions in which he dabbled.[1] Besides his wireless radio communication and alternating current systems, and like other great inventors from da Vinci to Edison, Tesla was intrigued by a great many other issues. One such issue to which he gave a great deal of thought was the relationship between matter and energy. Late in life he even claimed to have developed a new dynamic theory of gravity, though the details of his theory were never presented. One thing was clear, however, Tesla did not think that Albert Einstein had gotten it right when he introduced his theories of relativity: "Tesla continuously attacked the validity of Einstein's work," O'Neill would write, "he ridiculed the belief that energy could be obtained from matter."[2]

Einstein, of course, received the Nobel Prize in Physics in 1921 "for his services to theoretical physics, and especially for his discovery of the law of the photoelectric effect."[3] While he is probably best known for his development of "the world's most famous equation, $E = mc^2$," Einstein's greatest contributions were in reconciling the laws of classical

mechanics with the laws of electromagnetic fields.[4] Einstein believed that Newtonian mechanics did not adequately accomplish this reconciliation, which led to his special theory of relativity in 1905. Extending this concept to gravitational fields, Einstein published his general theory of relativity in 1916. The following year he applied the general theory to model the structure of the universe as a whole.

To vastly oversimplify, general relativity provides for a unified description of gravity as a geometric property of space and time. One key feature is that space-time is both curved and a function of the energy and momentum of matter and radiation.[5] This is why light is bent around planets and other celestial bodies as it is influenced by their gravitational fields. It is also why time passes more slowly the closer the clock is to the source of gravitation (or conversely, why astronauts on a mission to points outside our solar system would return much younger than if they had remained on Earth).

Undeterred by the worldwide preeminence of such a man as Einstein, Tesla, at the ripe old age of eighty-two, wrote that he was fortunate enough to work out "two far reaching discoveries." One was a dynamic theory of gravity, which he said "explains the causes of this force and the motions of heavenly bodies under its influence so satisfactorily that it will put an end to idle speculation and false conceptions, as that of curved space." The "idle speculation" of curved space was, of course, one of the key features of Einstein's general theory of relativity. Tesla argued that Einstein's theories were nothing more than "magnificent mathematical garb which fascinates, dazzles and makes people blind to the underlying errors."[6]

Tesla's other far-reaching discovery was a physical truth that he felt could best be expressed by the statement:

"There is no energy in matter other than that received from the environment."

Opposite: Albert Einstein, ca. 1947

He argued that no theory could

"explain the workings of the universe without recognizing the existence of the ether and the indispensable function it plays in the phenomena."[7]

The presence of the ether—the unseen medium between all the bodies of the universe—had already been contested by many scientists, including Einstein. Instead of the ether, Einstein inserted his own space-time construct that allowed space to curve around gravitational bodies.[8] Tesla disagreed with Einstein, saying:

"I hold that space cannot be curved, for the simple reason that it can have no properties. It might as well be said that God has properties. He has not, but only attributes and these are of our own making. Of properties we can only speak when dealing with matter filling the space. To say that in the presence of large bodies space becomes curved is equivalent to stating that something can act upon nothing. I, for one, refuse to subscribe to such a view."[9]

The question was not inconsequential—if the ether existed then the speed of light would not be constant, it would vary depending on the forces of the celestial bodies. Experiments carried out by Albert Michelson and William Morley in 1887 had already shown that the ether actually did not exist, notwithstanding Tesla's insistence many decades after this to the contrary.[10]

Still undeterred, Tesla believed that he had discovered what came to be known as "Tesla waves," which would move faster than the speed of light. He argued that the propagation of currents from his magnifying transmitter—"a peculiar transformer specially adapted to excite the Earth"[11]—would begin with "a theoretically infinite speed" and then later "proceeds [*sic*] with the speed of light." But that would not be the end as "from there on it again increases in speed, slowly at first, and then more rapidly," eventually passing through the Earth to a point diametrically opposed to it "with approximately infinite velocity."[12] Needless to say this was a direct contradiction to Einstein's demonstration that the speed of light is a constant and that nothing can travel faster than the speed of light, at least in a vacuum.[13]

Whether Tesla could have provided some additional insight to Einstein's thinking on relativity if he had presented his views many years earlier we will never know. In the end it was Einstein whose theories were written down, underwent scrutiny, and are generally accepted today.

This apparent animosity for Einstein may have been one-sided as Einstein seems not to remember Tesla that much. This was evidenced on Tesla's seventy-fifth birthday party (in 1931), which unlike the non-events of most of his earlier birthdays, was something of a marvel for Tesla, who by that time had become largely secluded in his New Yorker hotel room. Kenneth Swezey had arranged to have famous engineers and scientists from all over the world send something to Tesla. Letters and tributes flooded in, including those from Nobel laureates Robert A. Millikan, William H. Bragg, E.V. Appleton, Arthur H. Compton, and even Albert Einstein. The note from Einstein simply congratulated Tesla on his contributions to the field of high-frequency currents, seemingly forgetting all of the other Tesla achievements. This slight probably went unnoticed, however, as *Time* magazine put Nikola Tesla on the cover.[14]

Along with the cover story were more than seventy congratulatory letters, which were mounted and presented to Tesla in the form of a testimonial volume. As would be expected, most lavished praise on Tesla for his accomplishments. *Science* editor and publisher Hugo Gernsback nearly gushed, writing:

"If you mean the man who really invented, in other words, originated and discovered—not merely improved what had already been invented by others—then without a shade of doubt Nikola Tesla is the world's greatest inventor, not only in the present but in all history... His basic as well as revolutionary discoveries, for sheer audacity, have no equal in the annals of the intellectual world."[15]

All was good for Tesla. Sadly, over the remaining dozen years of his life he would become largely forgotten as others—notably Edison, Westinghouse, and Marconi—got credit for Tesla's actual contributions.

Above: Bladeless turbine

Bladeless Turbines

When he was not taking on Einstein, Tesla was thinking about some of the fundamental "truths" of science. In one case he disagreed with the idea that turbines needed to have blades like a propeller to catch the air or water as they moved in a particular direction. Tesla had experimented with what would come to be called the bladeless turbine as far back as his youth when he played with waterwheels of his own invention. His updated version of a bladeless turbine could be used, Tesla mused, to power "automobiles, locomotives and steamships," not to mention airplanes and ocean liners, all new creations of the modern world of the early twentieth century.[16]

Tesla had begun working on bladeless turbines when he was consulting with the Westinghouse Company in Pittsburgh, but this project, like so many others, was put on hold while he toiled on his alternating current designs of high potential and high frequency. But in 1906 he gave himself a fiftieth birthday present by demonstrating his bladeless turbine in public. The basic design of the turbine relies on the principle of boundary layer flow, that is, where the movement of the liquid or gas passes over a series of smooth disks. Some of the liquid or gas adheres to the disks, which creates a vortex that spirals toward the center and spins the turbine. Tesla described it in an interview with the *New York Herald* in 1911:

"Now, suppose we make this metal plate that I have spoken of circular in shape and mount it at its centre on a shaft so that it can be revolved. Apply power to rotate the shaft and what happens? Why, whatever fluid the disk happens to be revolving in is agitated and dragged along in the direction of rotation, because the fluid tends to adhere to the disk and the viscosity causes the motion given to the adhering particles of the fluid to be transmitted to the whole mass."[17]

This resulted in very large power output for a very small size and weight. Because no projecting blades were needed, the turbine could withstand much greater pressures.

Not-So-Practical Ideas

Not surprisingly, Tesla had some ideas over the course of his life that were not all that practical. Two such ideas were so grandiose that even Tesla could not have believed he could accomplish them. Still, he indulged his imagination both to stave off boredom and perhaps, to give himself the freedom to think beyond the norm. During his period of hiding in the mountains after his days in Graz, Tesla contemplated the construction and operation of a huge tube that would connect Europe and the United States. The purpose of this tube? Merely to transport mail, which would be done in "spherical containers" pushed through the tube by water pressure. While this may have seemed like a frivolous exercise to many, his mental calculations dealt with the problem of friction of the water in the tube, a key problem solved that would later be put into force with the invention of his bladeless turbine.[18]

During this same period of his early life, Tesla also used the development of another completely impractical idea as a way to work through key mathematical and physical problems that would later help him devise more realistic inventions. Tesla proposed that a ring be built around the entire Earth. Constructed with a system of scaffolding encircling the equator, Tesla supposed that once in place the scaffolding could be removed and the ring would hover in space "rotating at the same speed of the Earth." Perhaps this could be exploited as a sort of "high-speed moving platform" for rapid transport if, for example, the ring could be held still while the Earth turned under it "at a speed of 1,000 miles per hour." Tesla never marketed this idea.

Flying Machines

Like da Vinci, Tesla had visions of creating flying machines. Since the Wright brothers had made the first practical, powered heavier-than-air flight in 1903 the development of airplane technology had proceeded rapidly. Fixed-wing aircraft, mainly biplanes, were widely used in World War I by both sides of the conflict. Never satisfied with standard airplanes, Tesla put his efforts into inventing a completely "new type of flying machine," which he called a "helicopter-plane." Tesla's plan was to build a precursor to what we today call a vertical takeoff and landing (VTOL) aircraft:

"The invention consists of a new type of flying machine, designated "helicopter-plane", which may be raised and lowered vertically and driven horizontally by the same propelling devices and comprises: a prime mover of improved design and an airscrew, both especially adapted for the purpose, means for tilting the machine in the air, arrangements for controlling its operation in any position, a novel landing gear and other constructive details, all of which will be hereinafter fully described."[19]

The plane would look and act like no other plane. After rising from the ground vertically, the pilot would tilt the plane forward while his seat tilted to maintain an upright position and the wings repositioned horizontally. Besides the unique system for both vertical and horizontal

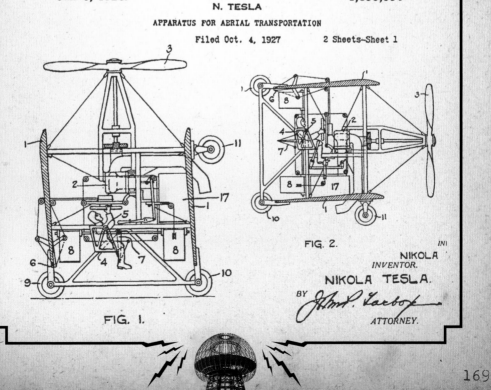

Jan. 3, 1928.   1,655,114

N. TESLA

APPARATUS FOR AERIAL TRANSPORTATION

Filed Oct. 4, 1927   2 Sheets—Sheet 1

FIG. 1.

FIG. 2.

NIKOLA
INVENTOR.

NIKOLA TESLA.

BY

ATTORNEY.

propulsion, the helicopter-plane was also one of the first attempts to use turbine engines in rotor aircraft. Tesla may have been thinking of this technology for even more broadly useful purposes; he may have traveled to Detroit to market his design as a "flying automobile."[20]

Unfortunately, the aircraft idea was not further developed and became, in 1928 when he was seventy-two years of age, the last patent Tesla would receive.

Shadowgraphs and X-Rays

Tesla readily acknowledged that X-rays had been discovered by German physicist Wilhelm Röntgen, even though he had already experimented with what he called "shadowgraphs" several years earlier. He had alluded to this during his lecture tour in 1892 when he described "visible black light and a very special radiation." Like radio and so many other discoveries Tesla was working on, his shadowgraph research was interrupted by the fire that destroyed his laboratory in the spring of 1895. Still, when in the fall of that same year Röntgen announced his discovery of Röntgen rays, commonly called X-rays, Tesla was immediately able to send shadowgraph pictures taken with his "very special radiation." Röntgen was very much impressed, responding with "the pictures are very interesting. If you would be so kind as to disclose the manner in which you obtained them."[21]

Tesla joined the other luminaries in the field—Thomas Edison, Michael Pupin, Oliver Lodge, and others—in refocusing his research on this marvelous, and intimidating, new field. But Tesla's "X-rays" were different—while others were using Röntgen-type tubes at low strength and at close range, Tesla was "taking photographs through the skull at a distance of forty feet from the tube."[22] Over the next two years or so Tesla published prolifically on his X-ray research, taking "through the body" photos of various small animals, his assistants, and even himself.[23] At first Tesla and others believed that Röntgen rays could be used in experimentation quite safely. Thomas Edison even shot X-rays directly into his own eyes and those of an assistant, Clarence Dally, using his fluoroscope invention. Dally later died of injuries related to these poisonous doses of radiation and Edison himself nearly lost his eyesight, prompting him later to exclaim, "Don't talk to me about X-rays, I am afraid of them."[24] Tesla also experienced odd physical ailments and pains, but it was only after an assistant received severe blistering of the skin and even raw exposed flesh that Tesla understood the risks and began warning that protection from radiation exposure was necessary.[25]

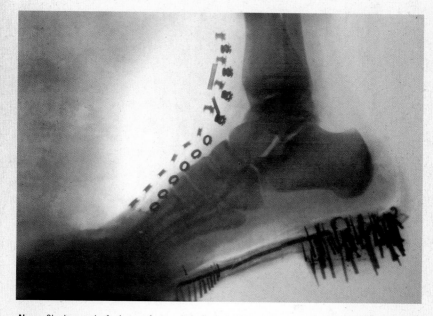

Above: Shadowgraph of a human foot made by Tesla in 1896 with X-rays generated by his vacuum tube

Radar

World War I began in Europe in 1914 and one of its first battles was the Battle of Kolubara, where Austria fought the Serbian army. Tesla, though naturalized as an American citizen in 1891, was still proud of his Serbian heritage and wanted to do something to help the cause. He had been experimenting with stationary waves for many years and believed that radio waves could be used to "determine the relative position or course of a moving object, such as a vessel at sea, the distance traversed by the same, or its speed."[26] Later, Tesla presented some of the first technical principles for radar. During a far-ranging interview published in *The Electrical Experimenter*, Tesla explained three separate schemes for using

Beginning: "My Inventions," by Nikola

FEB.
1919
20 CTS.

ELECTRICAL
EXPERIMENTER

SCIENCE AND INVENTIO

OVE
175
ILLUS

THE TESLA
WIRELESS LIGHT
SEE PAGE 692

electricity to locate submarines, more specifically the German U-boats being used during World War I.[27] In one, Tesla boasted:

"Now we are coming to the method of locating such hidden metal masses as submarines by an electric ray. If we can shoot out a concentrated ray comprising a stream of minute electric charges vibrating electrically at tremendous frequency, say millions of cycles per second, and then intercept this ray, after it has been reflected by a submarine hull for example, and cause this intercepted ray to illuminate a fluorescent screen (similar to the X-ray method) on the same or another ship, then our problem of locating the hidden submarine will have been solved."[28]

Tesla also anticipated the modern radar that would be developed many years later in the run up to World War II.[29] In any case, Tesla's ideas for using underwater radar turned out to be impractical for technical reasons, and later the military would opt for a sonar technique that uses sound propagation to echo-locate underwater objects.

There have been many other discoveries of which Tesla deserves at least some credit but likely receives little attention. A year after Tesla's death, O'Neill lamented the lack of credit his hero received:

"Tesla, thus, in one lecture reporting his investigations covering a period of two years, offered to the world—in addition to his new electric vacuum lamps, his highly efficient incandescent lamp, and his high-frequency and high-potential currents and apparatus—at least five outstanding scientific discoveries: 1. Cosmic rays; 2. Artificial radioactivity; 3. Disintegrating beam of electrified particles, or "atom smasher"; 4. Electron microscope; and 5. 'Very special radiation' (X-rays)."

At least four of these innovations, when "rediscovered" up to forty years later, won Nobel Prizes for others; and Tesla's name is never mentioned in connection with them.[30]

One thing that has become clear in the seventy years that have elapsed since O'Neill's biography is that Tesla is considered by many as having been treated unfairly both by his compatriots in science and by history. This apparent slight led to both an immediate suspicion of a plot to suppress Tesla's influence and fodder for a variety of conspiracy theories.

THE WASHINGTON HERALD, SUNDAY, MARCH 17, 1912.

WHAT of the FUTURE IN ELECTRICITY

Dr. Nikola Tesla Looks Forward to the Era When One Titanic Electrical Wireless Station Shall Supply Power for the World—Tells of Other Developments That We Have Good Reason to Expect.

NIKOLA TESLA.

WHAT did the year 1911 contribute to the electrical progress of the world?"

"What does the year 1912 promise in the same direction?"

These questions, asked of Dr. Nikola Tesla, brought forth the following response:

"While there has been no fundamental discovery announced during the year just past, progress has been steady and continuous. Almost insensibly great changes have been brought about in various departments.

"Probably the most important of these is the extension of electric transmission lines from hydro-electric central plants. Although the spectre of government restriction has had a deterrent effect on the development of this important in-

Mr. Tesla said:

"I suppose that just at this time aviation commands the attention of the world more than any other field. For ages it has been the passionate desire of man to invade the domain of the bird, and finally it has materialized. The advent of a new motor, simpler, lighter, more powerful and efficient, and absolutely reliable in its operation, will convert the flying machine from a toy or a show apparatus to a practical and useful vehicle.

"A promising departure has already been made by Dr. Tesla in this line, a description of his new motor having been given in scientific journals recently.

"Almost as fascinating," Dr. Tesla continued, "are the possibilities of the discoveries that have been made by Mme. Curie. Though it may be safely predicted that the dreams of the enthusiasts will not be realized, enough has been achieved already to justify great expectations for

of its use. As a matter of fact, the world has not even at this moment the faintest conception of the really great and valuable results in other fields that are sure to be obtained in the near future.

"Far more important than communication is the transmission of power wirelessly, which will be done for innumerable purposes. To it could be cheaply provided that would enable every vessel or vehicle either on land or the water or in the air to safely travel without compass or any other means of direction such as has heretofore been known. One such wireless plant would be sufficient for the needs of the whole world and the means of saving property and human lives.

One Central Plant

"Remember," Dr. Tesla emphasized, "that I am now only mentioning one application of wireless power. Just think what benefits could be derived in this particular phase of aerial development by the construction of one single plant from which all the flying machines of the world could be operated without fuel or other energy of any kind."

Turning to other subjects he said:—

"Entirely new fields have already been opened up to scientific research and inventive application, but still greater possibilities lie before us.

"Think only what it would mean to disintegrate matter into its primary constituents, thus giving rise to new effects and phenomena and liberating forces heretofore unknown! One of the consequences, perhaps not the most important, would be the inexhaustible supply of radium emanations.

"Since advancing this idea I have spent much time attempting to realize it by the application of great electrical forces, but although I have attained tensions of 20,000,000 volts, sufficient to tear off particles from the toughest steel, they were found inadequate to break up the atomic structure. I am confident, though, that it will be done eventually.

"Another item of infinite promise is that of intense cold, so ably and successfully explored by Sir James Dewar. The production of liquid oxygen and hydrogen, if economically effected, will be revolu-

lectual progress must ...... less continents."

"As to the utilization ..... am glad to say that I have decided upon forward ..... tion of my new gas to ..... gine, which will per ..... economical use of fu ..... possible.

Improving the .....

"The energy supp ..... through the sun's ray ..... it could be cheaply ..... it would meet all ..... though engines have ..... ated by power so de ..... to this end have per ..... chiefly because of ..... of the supply. I ..... that the true solu ..... direction.

"Telephoning the ..... cables is possible ..... accomplished long ..... electricians been t ..... section. The trou ..... mitting and rec ..... pecially the latter ..... and require stro ..... entailing great lo ..... the surrounding ..... causing unavoidab ..... impulses. Failu ..... the great mathe ..... telephone lines ..... heavy wire and ..... coils, which have ..... tension and red ..... in the wire.

"A further ex ..... sion has been e ..... so-called phant ..... two separated ..... and practical ..... induction coil ..... crudity of the ..... ing very ef ..... through the h ..... marine cables ..... their construc

"How about ..... that visible ..... of a wire as ..... over a wire?

"We ...... mission ..... The forme ..... well establish

N. TESLA.
TURBINE.
APPLICATION FILED JAN. 17, 1911.

1,061,206.

Patented May 6, 1913.

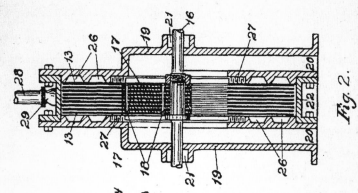

Fig. 2.

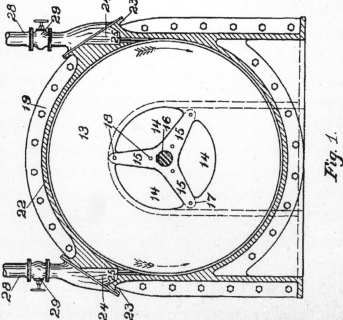

Fig. 1.

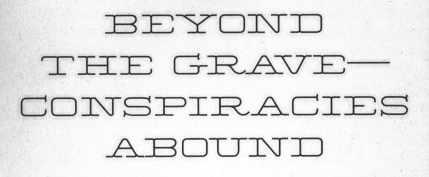

BEYOND
THE GRAVE—
CONSPIRACIES
ABOUND

Nikola Tesla was a brilliant, but also very eccentric, scientist with little affinity for the non-scientific drudgery of commercializing his inventions or properly handling his finances. Since his death he has become the quintessential "mad scientist" for many and a cult figure for others. This is in part due to Tesla himself, who had a habit of providing great copy for reporters. One day he was the cultured gentleman dressed impeccably and dining at the finest restaurants, the next a reclusive scientist hiding in his laboratory for days on end with very little sleep. Then he would be a showman on the lecture circuit, regaling the otherwise stodgy scientific community with his wireless light sabers and building-rattling oscillators. And of course there were the claims of wonderful, yet somewhat crazy, inventions ranging from communications with other planets, splitting the Earth down the middle, and death rays consisting of a "beam of matter moving at high velocity" that could destroy "10,000 airplanes at a distance of 250 miles."[1] The latter was actually called a "peace ray" by Tesla, who felt that it could also be used to form an "impenetrable, invisible wall of protection" that would make war "impossible" and act as an insurance of peace.[2]

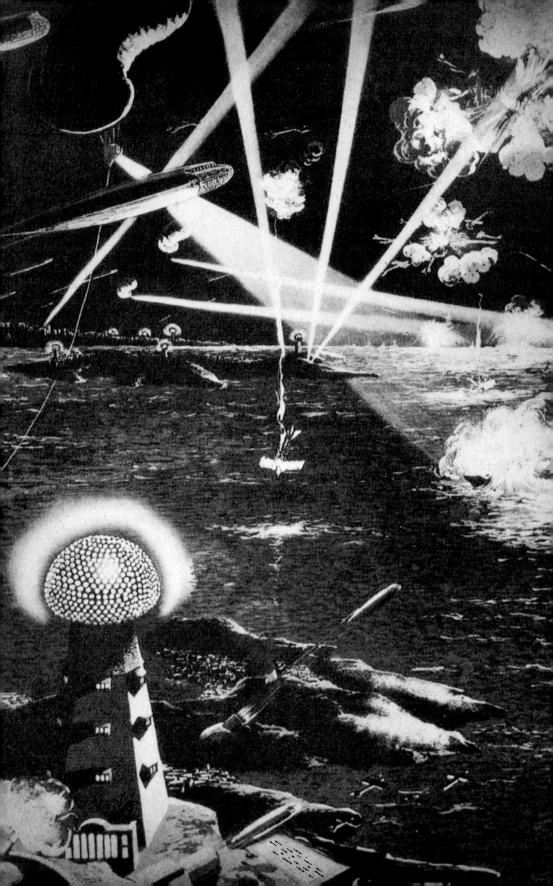

All of this, of course, positions Tesla's work perfectly for a wide range of conspiracy theories in the modern era.

During his illustrious career as an inventor Tesla developed many inventions that changed the world, including his unique design for a rotating magnetic field motor that enabled the use of alternating current on a commercial basis, wireless communication across vast distances, and even early "shadowgraphs," precursors to X-rays. He also made forays into other areas that, while he did not succeed in commercializing, set the stage for future developments, including wireless remote control of boats and other devices (robotics). Tesla made many grandiose claims that did not come to fruition. The biggest of these included the wireless transmission of power through the Earth and a directed energy weapon. He also claimed to have communicated with intelligent beings from the planet Venus or Mars.

Tesla died peacefully during the night of January 7, 1943. "The superman died as he had lived—alone," O'Neill writes. The local coroner declared his death to be from "natural causes incident to senility."[3] At nearly eighty-seven years old this would normally be the end of the story, but this was 1943 and the United States was in the midst of World War II. Everyone was suspicious of everyone and fears of spies infiltrating the populace were routine. O'Neill perhaps planted the initial seed for conspiracies to grow when he wrote "operatives from the Federal Bureau of Investigation came and opened the safe in his room and took the papers it contained, to examine them for a reported important secret invention of possible use in the war."[4] The stage was set for a series of mystery plays that continue to the present day.

Tesla's Stolen Papers

Playing into the hands of those predisposed to conspiracies, the government swept in to impound Tesla's key papers and trunks under the rather questionable authority of the U.S. Alien Property Custodian office. Since Tesla had become a naturalized U.S. citizen a full half-century before, the government's actions seemed as odd as Tesla's idiosyncrasies and phobias.

Opposite: The caption for this illustration from a 1922 issue of *Science and Invention* read: "War in the future as it will be conducted from the viewpoint of Tesla"

The heightened paranoia of the war-time period certainly increased the suspiciousness of the conspiracy theorists. As O'Neill alluded, the FBI did in fact have a "rather lengthy" file compiled on Tesla, which was not surprising given that Tesla was prone to bragging about super weapons that would end all war.[5]

Living a reclusive life for many years and without finances to maintain a laboratory, many of Tesla's papers were stored in a safe and in boxes in his small two-room suite at the New Yorker Hotel. Who knows what secrets were in those papers? According to theorists, the government knew, and they wanted the papers so that they could be gleaned for secret weapons . . . or to keep them from being stolen by the axis powers. Tesla's connections with arms merchants and communists through his Yugoslavian nephew, as well as a German propagandist, all raised the suspicions of various agencies interested in safeguarding the material.[6] Tesla's nephew, Sava Kosanovic, had managed to get an ailing Tesla to send a message to communist leader Marshall Tito supporting the unification of the Serb and Croat populations. Kosanovic also arranged for Tesla to meet with the exiled Yugoslavian king in New York.[7] While suspicions may have been warranted, it is unclear where Tesla was doing all of this secret research, since he rarely left his rooms in the latter part of his life, and when he did he was more likely to be feeding pigeons in Bryant Park than feeding secret information to the government. Tesla historian Marc Seifer discusses many of the fascinating details, including the activities of "ubiquitous surveillance mastermind" J. Edgar Hoover, but the core is that Tesla had built a working model of the "death ray" and hid it in his rooms. It was this death ray that the secret agents supposedly stole, along with Tesla's papers. They even went so far as to substitute an innocuous piece of electrical equipment found in every electrical laboratory.[8]

How much of this is reality and how much is fantasy is difficult to say, but the fact remains that his papers were taken and remained inaccessible for many years.

If one strips away the speculative portions of the story it loses a lot of its mystery. As one source puts it, the FBI file has been largely declassified and "makes for fascinating reading."[9] Indeed, Tesla did try to interest the U.S. government in a weapon of mass destruction,

Tesla's Latest Wonder.

Illustrating the Method by Which Electric Power Is Conducted From One Place to Another Without Wires. The Balloons Act as the Poles of the Dynamos and the Current Flashes Across Through the Rarefied Air.

Tesla's model transformer or "oscillator" in action when creating an effective electrical pressure of two and a half million volts. The actual width of space traversed by the luminous streams from the single terminal is over sixteen feet.

DIAGRAM ILLUSTRATING PRINCIPLE OF TESLA'S RECEIVER OF ELECTRIC POWER.

C—Primary coil.
D—Secondary coil.
D—Revolving terminal supported by balloon.
M—Lamps and motors energized by transmitted current.

... without loss through the air direct to a distant point, where it may be used for light or power. A comprehension of this invention depends upon an understanding of "voltage."

An electric current may be large in quantity and low in intensity or small in quantity and high in intensity as a stream of water large in volume and slow of motion or may be small and rapid. A stream of water an inch in diameter will exert more power than a small river if the pressure is great enough.

In handling electricity quantity is reduced to intensity and the reverse by means of "transformers." In the long-distance transmission of power the energy is transformed to a high intensity of voltage and then sent over the wires, and where it is received it is again transformed to a lower voltage and greater quantity for use.

Here is another preparatory illustration. Most people have seen electric sparks jump from one brass ball to another in electrical apparatus. The distance these sparks will jump depends not on the amount of electricity generated but on its intensity or voltage.

Now, there are two things which mainly underlie Tesla's new scheme. One is the production of voltages before hardly dreamed of, and the other is the increased conductivity of the air when it is rarefied as it is at high altitudes.

Up to date 15,000 volts has been the measure of the intensity at which electric power has been transmitted over copper wires, though now they are talking of doubling it. Tesla proposes to transmit it without wires at 1,500,000 volts or more. At this voltage a given quantity transmitted would produce about 300 times the ordinary amount of power when reduced with transformers.

It is a well-known laboratory fact that rarefied air is a conductor of electricity, though one of much resistance. The Crookes tube or X ray fame depend on this principle. With one sweep ...

Tesla takes this principle from the laboratories where, only, men have put it to use, and goes up to the clouds with it. He produces a wonderful voltage that will jump an enormous distance in every-day air, and proposes to take it in balloons up to where the air is a sort of natural Crookes tube. In such an altitude it will jump long distances to another terminal, he says, the layer of heavy air below being a non-conductor and resisting it like the rubber wrapping of a wire, for ordinary air is not a good conductor.

Tesla is the pioneer of high voltages. Some time ago he invented an "oscillator," a pump Tesla contrivance, for this purpose. He has been making them bigger and bigger and his last one gets up to 1,500,000 volts. The accompanying illustration shows his latest oscillator in action.

The diagrams illustrate the theory of the apparatus. In the transmitting apparatus A is an insulated high tension coil about a magnetic core. C is a second coil of larger wire. The terminals of both coils are shown. G is the generator or source of current. D is a balloon acting as a terminal itself or a terminal supported by a balloon to which the current passes. The current is supposed to pass thru this rarefied upper air from D to Di, a receiving balloon at a great distance. The primary and secondary coils of the receiving apparatus in the reverse of the transmitter. L and M indicate lamps and motors to be energized by the transmitted current.

In the long descriptive text accom...

SIX POLAR EXPEDITIONS.

Mr. Wellman's Polar Expedition.

Mr. Wellman's ship, the Fridtjof, has returned from Franz Josef Land, bringing news of the expedition down to August 2. Writing to us on that date, the leader announced the landing of his party at Cape Tegetthoff, and his proposed start for the north a few days later. The voyage to Franz Josef Land had been a successful one. After ten days in the ice Cape Grant was reached on July 27, Cape Flora on the 28th. Here the ship was turned back by ice, reaching Cape Tegetthoff on the 30th, after which the tour of Wilczek and Salm Islands was made before the final landing was effected. A house, named "Harmsworth House," on the inner shelf was taken from Cape Flora, had been erected at Cape Tegetthoff, but, in spite of the temptation to winter there, Mr. Wellman hoped to be able to adhere to his original plan and push northward to Crown Prince Rudolf Land, wintering there in an improvised hut of stones and snow. The house at Cape Tegetthoff would be of use to fall back upon in case of need.

German Expedition to the Arctic Seas.

The Helgoland, Captain Rüdiger, with the German Arctic expedition under Herr Theodor Lerner on board, returned in August to Hammerfest without having discovered any trace of Andrée's expedition. Some geographical work has been accomplished in the neighborhood of King Karls Land, which, according to published statements, was found to consist of three islands, viz.: Swedish foreland, Jena ...

... principle that causes an X ray to glow even when removed several feet from the static machine. But whatever it is it is one of the greatest wonders of the age and surely destined to revolutionize warfare.

In speaking of his ship moving and handling inventions Tesla said:

"Hitherto the only means of controlling the movements of a vessel from a distance have been supplied through the medium of a flexible conductor, such as an electric cable, but this system is subject to obvious limitations, such as are imposed by the length, weight and strength of the conductor which can be practically used; by the difficulty of maintaining with safety the high speed of the vessel or changing the direction of her movements with rapidity; the necessity of effecting the control from a point which is practically fixed, and from many other drawbacks which are inseparably connected with such a system.

"The plan which I have perfected involves none of these objections, for I am enabled by the use of my invention to employ any means of propulsion to impart to the moving body or vessel the highest possible speed, to control the operation of its machinery and to direct its movements from either a fixed point or from a body moving and changing its direction, however rapidly, and to maintain this control over great distances without any artificial connections between the vessel and the apparatus governing its movements, and ...

... by Water Power Out in the Mountains.

DIAGRAM ILLUSTRATING THE PRINCIPLE OF TESLA'S TRANSMITTER OF ELECTRIC POWER.

A—Primary coil.
C—Secondary coil.
G—Source of electrical energy.
D—Terminal supported by balloon.

The Same Force Made to Run Factories, Street Cars and Lights in a City Miles Away.

...CREATING A DEATH BEAM THAT COULD DESTROY 10,000 PLANES AT ONCE.

sometimes called a "teleforce" weapon. Receiving no positive response, Tesla tried to interest various European governments. Most of the FBI file, however, deals with the arguments held by various self-avowed stakeholders over who should have access to Tesla's notes after his death. When the Office of Alien Property removed everything from Tesla's safe, it put them in a warehouse along with "more than thirty barrels of material belonging to Tesla" that had already been in storage.[10]

What followed was an extensive period of arguing over who should be able to keep the papers. The U.S. government apparently wanted to ensure there were no secret weapons that could get into the wrong hands, while relatives and representatives from the ever-changing homeland of Yugoslavia felt they should hold his belongings. Eventually Tesla's papers were sent to Belgrade to become part of what is now the Nikola Tesla Museum.[11]

No "death ray" was ever found.

Tesla Murdered by Nazis

Not to be outdone by the U.S. government conspiracists, another conspiracy theory is that Nikola Tesla did not actually die of natural causes—he was murdered by Nazi spies. "The reality of Tesla's murder," says one website, "was brought home to us after listening to [a] YouTube presentation."[12]

The story goes that a man by the name of Eric Berman told a friend that he discovered his former girlfriend was the daughter of ex-Nazi SS Commando Otto Skorzeny. "Quite by chance" he met the aging Skorzeny who supposedly had been living in the U.S. working as a carpenter under an assumed name and the protection of the CIA. This meeting apparently took place in the late 1990s, despite the fact that Skorzeny officially died in Spain two decades earlier from cancer of the spine. In any case, the storyteller claims to have heard a full confession from Skorzeny, who also gave him a "shoebox full of over one-hundred photographs to substantiate his claims." Skorzeny—officially fighting in the Soviet Union at the time, and in fact recuperating from shrapnel injuries to his head—had instead been in New York City and had personally suffocated Tesla.

Skorzeny and fellow Nazi Reinhard Gehlen had purportedly tricked Tesla into revealing "the full extent of his most important discoveries," presumably to avoid having to do patent searches and read the multitude of publicly available scientific papers Tesla had published. After murdering Tesla, Skorzeny and Gehlen then helped themselves to the contents of Tesla's safe and delivered the goods to Adolf Hitler (who, not surprisingly, also had lived well beyond his supposed death and took up ranching in Montana as late as 1997).[13]

The reason for the supposed murder was to gain access to Tesla's inventions and patents so they could be weaponized. Somehow the litigation over patent rights, something that was pretty common during that time period, was caused by the fact that many of Tesla's patents had fallen into the hands of the Nazis. Tesla, according to the story, would never achieve the financial success he deserved because his technology was "repeatedly stolen and sold to the German Nazis and other foreign governments."

Proof that Skorzeny and Gehlen had murdered Tesla was that he was found fully dressed in a solemn black suit, arms folded on his chest. Why the murderers would present him in such an obviously odd situation when they wanted their murder to be a secret is unknown, but in any case there is no record of Tesla being found in anything other than his normal bedclothes.

As with any good conspiracy theory, the story is laced with tremendous detail that sounds convincing. It includes the twist that former President George H.W. Bush was actually George H. Scherff, Jr., the son of George Scherff, longtime assistant, bookkeeper, and all-around helper of Nikola Tesla. Variants of the story assert that Scherff's real goal was to steal Tesla's research in order to help the Nazis destroy America. Needless to say, this took a great amount of forethought, given that the real George Scherff began his many decades association with Tesla long before the Nazis came to power.

Not surprisingly there is substantial information showing that this conspiracy is nothing more than wild imagination, perhaps growing organically with each new telling. But there is a possibility that it could all be true. After all, there are videos on YouTube.

Talking with Aliens

Tesla effectively planted the seed for this idea when, in 1896, he suggested that "the possibility of beckoning Martians was the extreme application of [my] principle of propagation of electric waves."[14] During his time in Colorado Springs Tesla worked diligently on wireless communication as he attempted to perfect his long-range transmission of radio waves. At the same time he was working on the development of his Tesla coil, periodically shooting large bolts of lightning across the sky. But did he also rekindle his idea of talking to Martians by picking up signals from a far-off planet?

8

NICOLA TESLA PROMISES COMMUNICATION WITH MARS.

NICOLA TESLA.

THE TIMES: RICHMOND VA. SU

trade for the year 1899, were nearly 42 millions pounds sterling, which shows good increase.

The British are more than ever paying heed to the "made-in-Germany" cry.

Bank Gave Way. The Italian Government is much perturbed over the covering in of a portion of the promenade known as the Lungotevere Anguillara, on the right bank of the Tiber between the Garibaldi and Cestio bridges, which subsided recently. Alarmed at the possible consequences of the subsidence, the authorities towards midnight ordered the evacuation of the houses in the immediate neighborhood. Next morning the whole stretch of the promenade, a quarter of a mile long, had disappeared, with the pavement, lamp-posts, and trees. Between the river and the gulf thus created stood the massive embankment of solid masonry constructed 15 years ago to prevent the city from inundation. Shortly before 11 A. M. the mass broke up and fell into the stream. The cause of the subsidence is, apparently, the imperfect character of the foundations of the embankment, which at that point, where the river bends sharply, is exposed to the full shock of the current. Owing to the timely precautions of the authorities no lives were lost, but the damage is estimated at several million lire. Consternation prevails among the municipal authorities, who fear lest the entire Tiber embankment, which cost some $25,000,000, may have been seriously undermined by the action of the water.

Religious Freedom. The Reichstag was occupied on Wednesday with the debate on the first reading of a toleration bill brought in by the Center or Clerical party. This bill seeks to secure complete religious freedom for all German subjects. In agreement with its provisions, religious bodies which are recognized by any of the German Governments would be entitled to practice their religion without let or hindrance throughout the whole Empire. All limitations placed upon the dispensation of the Sacrament and upon religious propaganda by the laws of particular States would be abolished. Religious societies (orders) would not require to obtain special permission for their foundation or for the exercise of their functions. This last provision involves, of course, the repeal of the law against the Jesuits.

Count von Buelow, the imperial chancellor, declined to support the bill on the ground that it interfered with the Constitutional rights of some of the federated States. But he expressed the hope that all religious inequality would soon disappear.

After a long discussion, in which representatives of all parties defined their attitude towards the bill, it was referred to a committee of twenty-eight members for further consideration.

Cardinal is Fined. Cardinal Langenieux, of Rheims, was recently fined two francs for refusing to obey an order of the Socialist Mayor, which prohibited religious processions on All Saints' Day. The size of the fine shows what the sympathies of the court were. Although it is too soon to

LEGISLATU NORTH

Will Not Get Do Aycock is

PLAN FOR HIS

A Large Escort Him from Golds Move For form

(Special Dispa
RALEIGH, N. C.
Assembly will har
lar work until a
The Senate Comi
nounced until yeste
has not read out
House. He expect
Monday.

Leaders in both
lily say that dow
be taken up just a
officials are instal
AYCOC
While the gene
inauguration of
and other State o
pleted, the work
so far advanced t
be announced. T
committee named
ernor Aycock wi
Monday afternoe
Governor-elect a
ing on the tra
o'clock. They v
two Goldsboro m
the Goldsboro B
A GRAN
At the depot h
he met by the
tion Committee
to the Governor
fast will be serv
held until 11 o
elect constitutio
At 11 o'clock
Yarbrough Ho
with the civic
the place of
weather permi
vised platform
Capitol.
OA
The oath of
Judge Walte
Court.
It is certa
thousand peop
rade. It is in
indications th
conditions the
visitors in th
A large num
General Asse

There are thousands of people living in
They were sent, those marvelous signals, by a human being living and thinking so far away from us, both in space

Tesla writes in his notes that late one night he was working in his laboratory and recorded some unusual signals. At first he thought they might be random noise, but then he observed that "the changes I noted were taking place periodically, and with such a clear suggestion of number and order that they were not traceable to any cause then known to me." Tesla was sure the variations were not caused by more familiar electrical disturbances such as those produced by the sun, the Aurora Borealis, or earth currents. He dismissed the later assertions of others who argued what he recorded was merely atmospheric disturbances.[15] No, what Tesla had observed was something else:

"It was some time afterward when the thought flashed upon my mind that the disturbances I had observed might be due to an intelligent control. Although I could not decipher their meaning, it was impossible for me to think of them as having been entirely accidental. The feeling is constantly growing on me that I had been the first to hear the greeting of one planet to another. A purpose was behind these electrical signals..."[16]

Tesla largely dropped the "talking with planets" idea once he returned to New York as he was busy with "more urgent work," such as getting funding for Wardenclyffe. But he did maintain a belief that "there would be no insurmountable obstacle in constructing a machine capable of conveying a message to Mars, nor would there be any great difficulty in recording signals transmitted to us by the inhabitants of that planet." Assuming, Tesla noted, that "they be skilled electricians."[17]

Interest in the theory was heightened by a Margaret Storm book called *Return of the Dove*. Later, another book by Arthur Matthews (*Wall of Light: Nikola Tesla and the Venusian Spaceship*) suggested that Tesla not only talked with extraterrestrials—he was one![18]

Whether Tesla did intercept some signals from Mars or Venus is highly doubtful, but it is safe to assume that the idea he was an actual Venusian is purely fictional. The more likely scenario is that he simply picked up random noise, or natural radio sources, or even signals from other researchers testing their radio transmissions.[19] In any case, this revelation led many people to acknowledge that Tesla was perhaps more than just a little eccentric. And while over time Tesla's idiosyncrasies became more profound, no further signals from extraterrestrial life on other planets have been received. At least as far as we know.

Tesla Shrugged?

A particularly interesting idea is that Ayn Rand's fictional character John Galt, from her seminal novel *Atlas Shrugged*, was at least partially patterned after Nikola Tesla.[20] After all, Galt had studied physics and became an engineer, then designed a revolutionary new motor powered by ambient static electricity."[21] Galt became frustrated when the company he worked at embraced collectivism and he walked out, leaving his new motor behind.

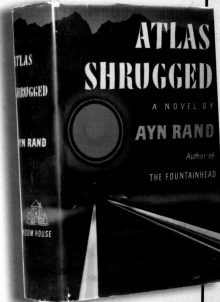

This story plays well with Nikola Tesla's actual history, at least when it is infused with some speculation that perhaps extends well beyond actual fact. Tesla obviously studied physics and became an electrical engineer. He designed a revolutionary new motor powered by alternating current and experimented with electrostatic electricity. And like Galt, Tesla became frustrated with the corporatism of working for Edison.

Rand even alludes to Tesla coils—"It was the coil that I noticed first . . . Those men, long ago, tried to invent a motor that would draw static electricity from the atmosphere, convert it and create its own power as it went along."[22] While there are clear departures from Tesla in the Galt character, these changes are certainly within the normal realm of creative writing. *Atlas Shrugged* is, after all, a novel.

The key to the thread is that John Galt, like Nikola Tesla, was interested in the production of what effectively would be "free energy." Virtually all costs associated with electrical power generation, transmission, and use would be eliminated. Tesla had discovered what he called "terrestrial stationary waves" in his laboratory in Colorado Springs. The Earth could transmit power—acting as a conductor that would be as responsive, and controllable, as a tuning fork. With this knowledge Tesla was able to light two hundred lamps without the use of wires. Returning to New York, Tesla planned to develop not only wireless communication in his new facility at Wardenclyffe, but also wireless power freely distributed to all through the Earth's surface.

With this as a base, the John Galt connection—creating free energy from static electricity—is sometimes extended to include Wilhelm Reich. Reich claimed to have discovered what he called "orgone," which was a physical energy contained in all living matter as well as in the atmosphere. He believed that this orgone could generate "free, useable energy."[23] Galt, Reich, and Tesla all discovered "free energy." So where is it? Why do we have to pay the electrical utility for our power and wait for them to get power back on after a storm? Well, according to the conspiracy theorist, it is because the few people with political and corporate power do not want the rest of us to take away their profits by having access to energy that is "free."

Left: Tesla coil
Opposite: Coils responding to electric oscillations

Suppression of "Free Energy"

One of the most enduring theories is that Tesla had discovered how to deliver "free energy" to everyone on the planet, and that this discovery was suppressed because the corporate powers could not then charge people for energy. Tesla did, in fact, work on how to obtain energy from cosmic rays, radiant energy, the Earth's electrostatic charge, and a variety of other natural sources. The story goes that Tesla managed to succeed in this endeavor just before his death, which admittedly strains credibility given Tesla's rapidly declining physical and mental health during this period. This, of course, is why the FBI broke into his hotel suite immediately after his death and took all his papers—to keep the public from gaining free energy.[24] Or death rays.

The free energy rationale is also the reason given for why J. Pierpont Morgan had withdrawn funding for Wardenclyffe—because he could not make money from free energy, and because he had invested in the

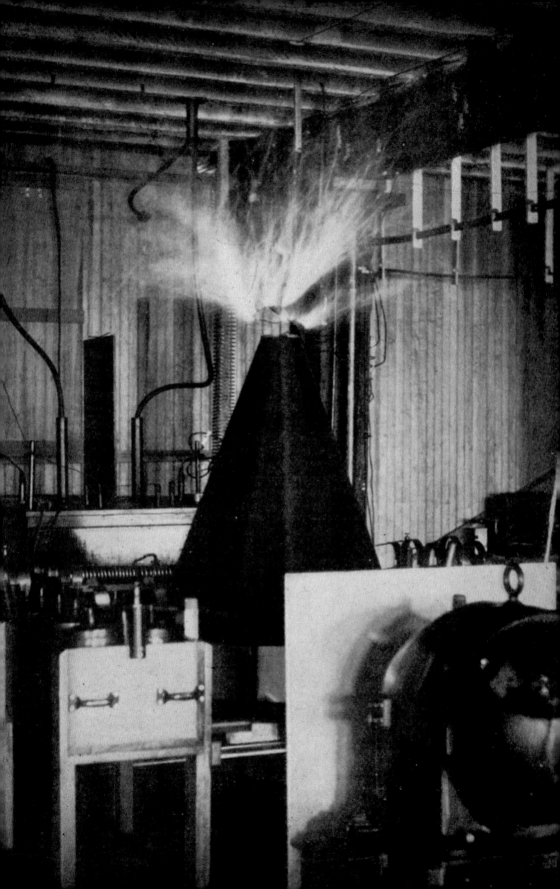

copper used for transformer coils and transmission lines. While Morgan was certainly a ruthless businessman, Tesla himself debunks the idea that Morgan shut down Wardenclyffe over free energy, saying that "it would have been most unreasonable to expect him to do anything more."[25]

Still, the idea that the government or the rich banker conspired to withhold universal free energy from the world is apparently too persuasive for its adherents to shrug off. Clearly if such a thing were possible it would eliminate our reliance on fossil fuels as we would have unlimited energy—and it would be free. Perhaps that is why this conspiracy theory has hung around for so long. People like the idea.

The idea has grown beyond the simple speculation that the government suppressed Tesla's inventions. One expanded version is explained in an hour-long video called "The Energy Lie (What the Energy Cartels Don't Want You to See)," which explains that a host of inventions by Tesla, Marco Rodin, Stan Meyers, and others have apparently been actively suppressed.[26] For the producers, the energy crisis is a lie and "the suppression of any technological advance can not be tolerated if we wish to be a 'civil'ization." Of course, the main reason for this suppression is greed, and "what is right is not always profitable."

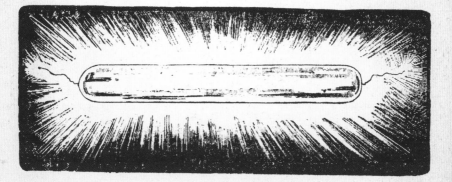

One problem with this thinking, however, is that Tesla never actually claimed to have created truly free energy. He was researching the potential for deriving energy from cosmic rays, that is, energy from the sun.[27] He also tried to harness the energy of the Earth with his project at Wardenclyffe. A large generator would be tuned to the harmonics of

Above: Newspaper illustration showing Tesla's "artificial light"
Opposite: Tesla's oscillator with purple streamers that were said to resemble seaweed at top of coil

the space between the Earth's surface and the ionosphere. The energy would form standing waves, such as those he claimed to have discovered in Colorado Springs, and then could be transmitted between towers around the world, thus filling this space with electromagnetic energy, from which anyone could "download" whatever energy they needed.[28] So the energy would not be "free" in the sense that no generation would be necessary, just in the sense that it could be "transmitted" and easily tapped without the need of wires or local electrical utilities.

Apparently Tesla's idea was neither technically plausible nor financially feasible. In the end the idea of relatively cheap, readily accessible energy did not come to fruition. But that will not stop the fans of "free energy" from complaining about its suppression. Then again, maybe one day we will find a way to have free energy. That idea of energy from the sun seems like a good place to start.

Playing the HAARP

One of the easiest ways to start a conspiracy theory is to have a secret program in a remote region run by a series of government agencies. Such a program actually does exist with HAARP, the High Frequency Active Auroral Research Program based in Alaska and funded by the U.S. Air Force, U.S. Navy, the Defense Advanced Research Projects Agency (DARPA), and the University of Alaska. Officially HAARP is "the premier facility for the study of ionospheric physics and radio science." The main project objective of HAARP is to understand the properties and behavior of the ionosphere so that they can "enhance communications and surveillance systems for both civilian and defense purposes."[29]

Okay, sounds a bit mysterious, but what does this have to do with Tesla? The idea is that HAARP has secretly perfected a particle-beam weapon (death ray) invented by Tesla, perhaps the one "stolen" by the FBI or Nazis immediately after his death. This ionospheric weapon would be able to shoot down enemy aircraft (or perhaps spacecraft) and ballistic missiles from Russia or elsewhere. Theorists go so far as to suggest a beam of electricity could destroy facilities anywhere on the planet, although it is unclear how this beam of electricity would deal with the curvature of the earth.[30] Tesla's death ray is not the only conspiracy involving HAARP, which has been blamed for triggering all manner of natural disasters as well as flipping Earth's magnetic poles, causing earthquakes, and manipulating weather.[31]

In reality, HAARP is a facility for doing research intended to understand natural ionospheric characteristics, so scientists can develop methods that mitigate these effects to improve the reliability or performance of communication and navigation systems. But death rays are a lot more interesting.

Tesla's Nobel Prize Was Stolen

Despite their combined productivity and influence on the future of modern electricity, neither Thomas Edison nor Nikola Tesla ever won

Opposite: HAARP ionispheric research facility, Gakona, Alaska

the Nobel Prize. There are those who say that the prize was "stolen" from Tesla because of Edison. But the reality was even more complex than the conspiracy.

Alfred B. Nobel had gained wealth and prominence for his invention of dynamite, an irony not lost on those issuing the Nobel Peace Prize. Nobel bequeathed that his estate should be used to create a series of prizes to those who confer the "greatest benefit on mankind" in several disciplines—physics, chemistry, physiology, medicine, literature, and peace. Each year a committee determines who in each discipline deserves the prize.

Tesla and Edison were picked to share the Nobel Prize for Physics in 1915. Or at least that is what was published in the *New York Times* on November 6 of that year, based on a Reuters' dispatch.[32] When approached by reporters, it became clear that neither Tesla nor Edison had received any official notice from the Nobel organization. Notwithstanding this rather obvious clue, the news spread like wildfire throughout the media, quickly "going viral" as we would say today. Unfortunately, the report turned out to be false. A few days later the Nobel committee awarded the physics prize to Sir William Henry Bragg and his son William Lawrence Bragg for their use of X-rays to determine the structure of crystals.[33]

Rumors at the time suggested that the Nobel committee had retracted the award due to the animosity between Tesla and Edison. There seems to be no evidence in support of this speculation, and the Nobel Prize committee would not have withdrawn an award based on rumors that the recipients intended to refuse it, especially since neither Edison nor Tesla had been informed of their selection. Oddly, O'Neill insists that while "the full story of what took place is not known…it is definitely established that Tesla refused to accept the award."[34] Despite this assertion from someone who knew Tesla, there is no corroborating support for it. The fact that O'Neill also gets the year of the non-award wrong—1912 instead of 1915—also brings into question his assertion.

Clearly Tesla and Edison had a complex professional relationship. Early on they occasionally dined together, but later, Tesla's winning

Opposite: Tesla near spiral coil, at his East Houston Street laboratory

of the war of the currents, the Chicago Exposition successes, and the Niagara contracts would certainly give reason for Edison to limit his contact with Tesla.

Their personalities were also very different. Edison was self-educated while Tesla went to fine schools. Edison also was a trial–and–error man while Tesla was someone who thought out the theory in his head, sometimes for many years, before doing any experiment. When Edison died, Tesla noted that Edison:

"was inefficient in the extreme, for an immense ground had to be covered to get anything at all unless blind chance intervened and, at first, I was almost a sorry witness of his doings, knowing that just a little theory and calculation would have saved him 90% of the labor."[35]

In reality it appears to be simply a case of the media getting a false report and running the story in their best "Dewey Defeats Truman" moment before checking the facts. In any case, this was yet another incidence of Tesla coming close to a Nobel Prize but not getting one. In 1901 Wilhelm Röntgen received the Nobel Prize for his discovery of X–rays even though Tesla's work with "special radiation" had predated Röntgen's work. In 1909 Guglielmo Marconi received the Nobel Prize for his invention of radio, though years later it was determined that it was actually Tesla who had made the seminal invention. Then, in 1934, Frederick Joliot-Curie, who was a son–in–law of Marie Curie (winner of two Nobel prizes), won a Nobel Prize for discovering artificial radioactivity, which Tesla had described three decades before, but for which he received no credit or acknowledgment.[36]

There are many more conspiracy theories inspired both by Tesla's amazing inventions and his cornucopia of oddities. These conspiracy theories join his actual scientific theories as part of the legacy of the great inventor.

(No Model.)

N. TESLA.
ALTERNATING MOTOR.

No. 555,190.   Patented Feb. 25, 1896.

Fig. 1

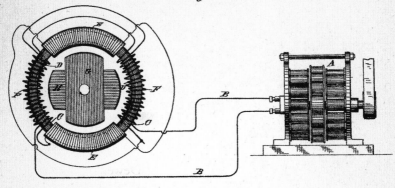

Fig. 2

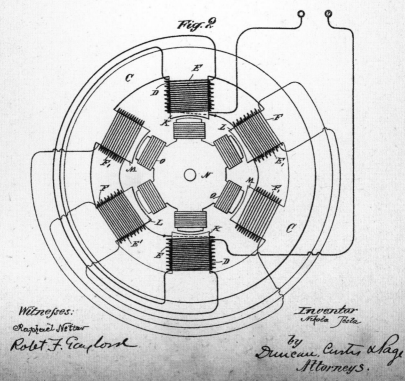

Witnesses:

Raphaël Netter

Robert F. Gaylord

Inventor
Nikola Tesla

by
Duncan, Curtis & Page
Attorneys.

CHAPTER
AMPERE
9

A LASTING
LEGACY

Tesla died in a lonely two-room suite—Room 3327 on the thirty-third floor, appropriately divisible by three—at the New Yorker Hotel in midtown Manhattan, not far from Penn Station and Madison Square Garden. This was just a few months before the Supreme Court upheld his original patent and gave Tesla credit for invention of the radio. Unfortunately for Tesla, this was long after Marconi had received a Nobel Prize in 1909 on technological ideas "borrowed" from Tesla. While he had become a naturalized American citizen over a half-century earlier, Tesla's cremated remains now rest in a spherical "Tesla ball"–shaped urn at the Nikola Tesla Museum in Belgrade.[1]

Over the course of his nearly eighty-seven years he traveled from humble Serbian beginnings to the cultured streets of Budapest, Paris, and New York, and then on to what was arguably one of the greatest eras of invention this nation has ever seen. And then, while he still longed to contribute to the greater good of the world, Tesla's achievements—and Tesla himself—faded into distant memory and seclusion. O'Neill noted that:

199

"Tesla was prolific in opening up vast new empires of knowledge. He showered his discoveries on the world at such a rapid rate and in such a nonchalant manner that he seems to have benumbed the minds of the scientists of his age. He was too busy to spend time developing the technical or commercial applications of each new discovery—there were too many other new and important revelations within his vision that must be brought to light. Discoveries were not happenstance events to him. He visualized them far in advance of their unfolding in the laboratory."[2]

While he may not get all the credit he deserves for his contributions, he did in fact contribute significantly to the betterment of mankind. His inventions, improvements of inventions, and innovative ideas for principles that would develop into the inventions of others include:

- An improved loudspeaker for the nascent telephone
- Rotating magnetic field
- A complete alternating-current system of dynamos, transformers, and motors that are the basis for today's electrical grid
- Alternating current induction motor
- Hydroelectric generator system at Niagara Falls
- Tesla coil
- Wireless telegraphy (radio)
- Neon and other fluorescent lights
- Vacuum tubes
- Wireless lighting
- The basic principles of radar
- Shadowgraphs and the basic principles of X-rays
- The rotary engine
- Bladeless turbine
- Remote control (radio-operated) weapons, boats, and submarines
- The basis for robotics (teleautomatons)
- Designs for a vertical takeoff and landing (VTOL) airplane
- Particle beam (laser) weaponry
- Standing waves / ionospheric energy transmission[3]

Opposite: Robert Underwood Johnson holding a loop with incandescent lamp, Tesla at the switch

There is no question that Tesla was far ahead of his time. Many of his ideas seemed to be impractical or even delusional or irrational. And perhaps many of his ideas did fit this description. Then again, perhaps all great inventors become great inventors in part because of their willingness to let their visionary ideas fly beyond rationality. Edison, Tesla, and virtually all others made many jaunts down the wrong road before finding the path to the future. When Tesla was developing his grandiose ideas for a World Wireless System at Wardenclyffe, he also fancied the idea that:

"[a]n inexpensive receiver, not bigger than a watch, will enable [any telephone subscriber] to listen anywhere, on land or sea, to a speech delivered or music played in some other place, however distant."[4]

While still in Budapest, Tesla had developed a loudspeaker or amplifier that was a precursor to today's wireless telephones. He did not patent the invention at the time. Later he told Katharine Johnson that "the time will come" that "by means of a pocket instrument and a wire stuck in the ground, you can communicate from any distance with friends from home through an instrument similarly attuned."[5] One hundred years later, we take for granted our smartphones as we wirelessly communicate

anywhere with anyone or listen to music delivered from satellites beaming radio signals from all over the world.

Probably the one invention most identified with him is the Tesla coil. This high-voltage, high-frequency, low-current resonant transformer had been used by Tesla for everything from lighting to power generation to X-ray shadowgraphs to wireless telegraphy. Its use as a power source for high-frequency lighting was a precursor to present-day compact fluorescent lightbulbs. Later the Tesla coil laid the foundation for modern-day radio[6] and was used commercially for radio into the 1920s.[7] Besides use for lightning research, energy from the coils also became "an essential medical device to easily warm up lower body tissues," and also, occasionally, an electrosurgical instrument that cauterizes the cut instantly to limit blood loss.[8]

Today, however, Tesla coils are mostly used for entertainment and educational purposes. Tesla coils of up to 1.5 million volts can be found in many science museums around the world, mainly because of their impressive lightning flashes that thrill children and adults alike. There has also grown a flourishing hobby industry around building Tesla coils—the proponents are called "coilers"—and they meet at "coiling" conventions to display their homemade Tesla coils.[9] Tesla coils have even made it to the world of professional hockey. The Tampa Bay Lightning of the National Hockey League installed a unit that drops down from above as the hockey rink is darkened, then shoots lightning bolts as the home team players are introduced.[10]

Pop Culture

Tesla, and his coils, have always inspired followers in the pop culture realm. Nikola Tesla has become, and remains, a pop culture idol in the United States and elsewhere. Besides the usual documentaries of long-dead scientists, Tesla appears in a variety of books, comics, movies, and television and radio programs. Tesla coils have been used to create electronic music by capturing the rate and duration of radio frequency cycles. Tesla coil-created music has been used by such artists as Björk

Previous: Double exposure publicity photo of Tesla in Colorado Springs laboratory, 1899

and Arc Attack.[11] The rock band Tesla took its name from the great electrician, and called their first album *Mechanical Resonance* after events related to the life of Nikola Tesla. Their follow-up album was called *The Great Radio Controversy* in reference to the conflict over who really invented radio—Marconi who got the recognition (and the Nobel Prize) or Tesla whose prior contributions were forgotten until long after the history books ingrained Marconi in our memories.[12]

Prefer new age music? Check out *Balkan Routes Vol. 1: Nikola Tesla*, released in 2011.[13] Into Russian synthetic pop and new wave music? Try out the band Tesla Boy (www.teslaboy.com), which was named after a song about a boy who could conduct electricity but who could not control it.[14] Feel like dancing to Tesla? Check out the dance beat of *Nikola Tesla at the Wardenclyffe Tower*, by Mademoiselle Bistouri and Daniele Santini.[15] How about opera? An appropriately very different kind of aria was written and performed by Jessica Lennick and Daniel Paul Lawson in 2010. They describe their inspiration:

"A staunch believer in the connection between his genius and sexual abstinence, Tesla shunned women, choosing instead to feed and care for pigeons in his hotel room at the New Yorker. His closest friend was a white dove that visited him every day at his hotel room window. In moments of delirium, Tesla believed this pigeon to have mystical knowledge and the ability to communicate with him, and declared to friends that he was in love with her. One night, the bird flew into Tesla's room close to death, and according to Tesla, a light brighter than anything he had created in his laboratory shone from her eyes before she died in his arms. Tesla said that at that same moment, he knew his life's work was finished."[16]

Not into music? A quick search of Amazon.com reveals you can buy a multitude of Tesla-related toys and games, including a Nikola Tesla "Oddbobbles" bobblehead figure statue (complete with handheld

Tesla coil), a Nikola Tesla finger puppet, and Nikola Tesla puzzles. You can even buy a fifty-thousand-volt working Tesla coil for only $229.[17] Want a Tesla T-Shirt? You can choose from a selection of almost thirty designs![18] Or pick up your Topps Mayo Nikola Tesla collectible football cards (selection of five styles).[19] There are also various posters, mugs, cups, wall clocks, prints, cardboard cutouts a full 78-inches tall, and of course your selection of Nikola Tesla Purple Positive Energy Plates for your home or kitchen. How about a handmade chair made from recycled and specialty woods—complete with Nikola Tesla graphics painted on front and back?[20] And do not forget your Tesla mouse pad for the office (or laboratory) computer. Gamers? Download the apps for your smartphone!

Tesla Goes to the Movies

When it comes to movies, Tesla has become a character or inspiration in a variety of popular films. And if the man himself is not a key player, his Tesla coil steals the scene. The most memorable is perhaps the Tesla coils that shoot bolts of lightning around the laboratory, circling the castle, and most stimulatingly, into the body of the monster to bring it to life in the classic Boris Karloff film *Frankenstein*.[21] Tesla, although seventy-five years old and reclusive when the 1931 film came out, is said to have built at least one of the Tesla coils for the movie. Ironically, Karloff was so afraid of being electrocuted that he refused

to do the scene where the monster is brought to life—the electrical effects designer Kenneth Strickfaden had to stand in for him.[22]

Tesla is a key character in the 2006 film *The Prestige*, starring Hugh Jackman, Christian Bale, Scarlett Johansson, and

Michael Caine.[23] In keeping with his rock-star status, Nikola Tesla is played by none other than David Bowie (who was also said to have patterned his extraterrestrial character after Tesla in *The Man Who Fell to Earth*).

The Prestige centers on the competition between two turn-of-the-twentieth-century magicians, each vying for fame and fortune in the emerging, yet surprisingly cutthroat, world of magic. Each tries to outdo the other in developing new tricks, and when one rival appears able to be in two places at once, the other seeks out the mysterious Nikola Tesla, then working in his remote Colorado Springs laboratory. At first, the "magic" of Tesla's electronic machine cannot be found. Or can it? Soon the secret is revealed to the magician and Tesla alike, but not to the filmgoing audience. Ultimately, Tesla's magic seems the most amazing of all, a magic that neither magician could replicate on his own.

On television you can catch Nikola Tesla the part-human, part-vampire scientist on the science fantasy series, *Sanctuary*.[24] The show followed the efforts of Dr. Helen Magnus to protect the "abnormals," a group of cryptics, legends, and abnormal animals/people" with extra-ordinary powers. The Nikola Tesla character, perhaps not surprisingly, has the ability to control electricity. When not sipping on the blood of the humans he despises, the fictional Tesla enjoys the taste of fine red wine. His adventures include being killed, then un-killed, as well as curing the dreaded Lazarus virus, infecting rich teenagers with a formula that slowly turns them into vampires, and then leading the government's anti-abnormal task force headquartered at the ubiquitous Area 51. The real Nikola Tesla would likely have been amused. Or perhaps not.

On the smaller screen, that is, YouTube, there are hundreds of videos featuring Tesla or his inventions. They range from traditional documentaries to conspiracy theories to tributes to the almost forgotten inventor of radio and Tesla coils. One of the most unique homages to Tesla is one by master illusionist Marco Tempest, which he did as part of the TED series of talks.[25] Tempest uses the principles of tanagra theater (a popular technique in the early twentieth century), which employs a series of mirrors to transform the image of an actor offstage and project a tiny version onstage. The result is that Tempest and his creative team combine sophisticated computer-generated projection mapping with an equally intricate pop-up book to tell the story of Nikola Tesla—"the greatest geek who ever lived."[26] Tempest uses his incredible imagination, marvelous stage presence, and high-tech displays to bring Tesla to life, through his amazing discoveries, and his trials and tribulations. All in a most entertaining five minutes.[27]

Energy from Nature

"It seems that I have always been ahead of my time."[28]

Throughout his life Tesla was interested in the power of nature. He used the natural energy of May bugs to power his stick windmill as a child. He helped harness the hydroelectric power of Niagara Falls with his alternating current motors and transformers. And he often spoke of harnessing the energy of the sun, stating that fossil fuels were wasteful. As far back as 1891 he argued that "nature has stored up in the universe infinite energy." To Tesla, "the eternal recipient and transmitter of this infinite energy is the ether." That particular idea did not hold up to scrutiny, but he continued to look to nature.[29] One of the most thought-provoking documents of Tesla's numerous writings was an article he wrote for *The Century Illustrated Magazine*, June 1900, which was edited by Robert Underwood Johnson. In a long and sometimes mystical treatise called "The Problem of Increasing Human Energy (with special references to the harnessing of the sun's energy)," Tesla leapt ahead a hundred years in anticipating the need for renewable sources of energy to power our planet.[30] He noted that "besides fuel, there is abundant material from which we might eventually derive power" and suggested that "an immense amount of energy is locked up in limestone, for instance, and machines can be driven by liberating the carbonic acid through sulfuric acid or otherwise." He even claimed to have constructed such an engine and that "it operated satisfactorily."

Tesla was so far ahead of his time that, while others at the turn of the twentieth century were busy exploiting coal, iron, aluminum, and drilling for oil, he was already recognizing the limits of those endeavors. He was into conservation. "Whatever our resources of primary energy may be in the future," Tesla wrote, "we must, to be rational, obtain it without consumption of any material."[31] He believed that natural sources of energy could "eliminate the need of coal, oil, gas or any other of the common fuels."[32]

One way was to harness the power of the wind:

> "It is difficult to believe, but it is, nevertheless, a fact, that since time immemorial man has had at his disposal a fairly good machine which has enabled him to utilize the energy of the ambient medium. This machine is the windmill."[33]

Tesla believed that the power of the wind was "very considerable." He was not so keen on the potential of harnessing the tides and felt that any wave- or tide-motor would have "but a small chance of competing commercially with the windmill, which is by far the better machine, allowing a much greater amount of energy to be obtained in a simpler way." One hundred years later the wind turbine is increasingly becoming a mainstay of renewable energy generation.[34]

Long ago Tesla came to the conclusion that energy from the sun was both possible and a potentially unlimited resource. He saw two ways in which this could be achieved—"either to turn to use the energy of the sun stored in the ambient medium, or to transmit, through the medium, the sun's energy to distant places from some locality where it was obtainable without consumption of material."

There were tremendous technological challenges in the year 1900 to accomplish this vision, but Tesla believed the best option "to obtain

power would be to avail ourselves of the sun's rays, which beat the earth incessantly and supply energy at a maximum rate of over four million horsepower per square mile." He believed that "an inexhaustible source of power would be opened up by the discovery of some efficient method of utilizing the energy of the rays." While the development of capture and storage technologies for exploiting solar energy would take another one hundred years to reach a level of commercial feasibility, the man who could envision an entire alternating current transformer in his head also envisioned both the need and potential of tapping the energy of the sun.

These dreams of unlimited natural sources of energy brought Tesla into contact with other visionaries of nature. On various occasions, he had met the famous environmentalist John Muir while attending dinners at the Johnson's. Muir had befriended Robert Underwood Johnson years earlier. In fact, as an influential editor at *The Century Magazine*, Johnson had teamed with Muir to become a driving force behind the creation of Yosemite National Park in the Sierra Nevada mountain range of California in 1890. A decade later it was Johnson who encouraged Muir to start an association to protect the Sierra Nevadas. In 1892 Muir, with the help of Johnson and others, formed the Sierra Club.[35]

Tesla and Muir got along quite well. Tesla was enthralled with Muir's "magnificent description" of Yosemite Valley.[36] Muir appreciated that Tesla's inventions "sought to utilize renewable energy and minimize destruction of natural resources."[37]

Tesla was not finished dreaming up renewable energy sources. He hoped that one of the uses of his revolutionary bladeless turbine would be for development of geothermal power. In "Our Future Motive Power," published in *Everyday Science and Mechanics* in December 1931, Tesla describes how "the prospects of utilizing temperature differences in the ocean, solid earth or the atmosphere" could be exploited for useable energy.[38] "It is a well-known fact," Tesla had noted, "that the interior portions of the globe are very hot, the temperature rising, as observations show, with the approach to the center at the rate of approximately 1 degree C. for every hundred feet of depth." These simple temperature

Opposite: John Muir, 1902

differences, when transferred between two vessels, could drive the armatures of electrical generators. This would provide one way of "getting motive power from the medium without consuming any material."

Ever confident in his abilities, Tesla believed that "it is possible, and even probable, that there will be, in time, other resources of energy opened up, of which we have no knowledge now."[39] Tesla may not have always achieved his goals, but he set those goals far into the future.

Honors

Claimed as a "favorite son" by Croatia (the region where he was born), Serbia (his ethnic heritage), and the United States (where he lived for most of his life), Nikola Tesla has received a variety of honors from all over the world. While he was alive he received the prestigious Edison Medal from AIEE, the John Scott Medal from the city of Philadelphia, and several honorary doctorates.

In his honor the International System of Units elected to name the unit measuring magnetic field B (also referred to as the magnetic flux density and magnetic induction), the "Tesla" (T). The effect of wireless energy transfer to wireless powered electronic devices is known as the "Tesla Effect."[40]

At least two ships have been named after Tesla. The first was a Liberty ship named the USS *Nikola Tesla* that was launched only nine months after his death in 1943. The second boat is a scientific research vessel, the R/V *Tesla*, fielded by Aqua Survey, Inc., an ecotoxicology and geophysical survey company based in New Jersey.[41] According to Ken

Hayes,[42] President of ASI, because they "offer electromagnetic surveys that use coils to induce and then detect buried metallic objects" (e.g., unexploded bombs, pipelines, and treasure), "it was only fitting that we name our latest research vessel" after the man who helped develop the visions that made that technology possible.

Equally appropriate given his claims of extraterrestrial communication, a crater on the moon has been named after Tesla, and so has a minor planet. Back on Earth, the main airport for the capital of Serbia is named the Belgrade Nikola Tesla Airport. Serbia has also named a power plant after him. In Croatia, the Nikola Tesla Memorial Centre has been established in Tesla's home town of Smiljan, near Gospić. It includes a bust of Tesla designed by Ivan Meštrović, a friend of Tesla's.

In the United States, there are many tributes and memorials to Nikola Tesla. The U.S. Postal Service issued a commemorative stamp of Tesla and other scientists in the 1980s. In New York City, the corner of 40th Street and 6th Avenue near Bryant Park where Tesla roamed many a day feeding pigeons has a street sign labeling it "Nikola Tesla Corner." The Institute of Electrical and Electronics Engineers (IEEE) installed a plaque honoring Tesla on the façade of the New Yorker Hotel, Tesla's residence for the last decade of his life. IEEE also sponsors an annual Nikola Tesla Award given to "an individual or team that has made an outstanding contribution to the generation or utilization of electric power."[43]

Above: Nikola Tesla corner, 40th Street and Avenue of the Americas, New York City

Tesla's contribution to the development of the first hydroelectric plant at Niagara Falls is so great that there are not one, but two, statues erected in tribute to the Serbian-born naturalized American. The first monument to Nikola Tesla is located on Goat Island between the falls on the American side. It was a gift of the then Yugoslavian government to the United States in 1976. The work of Croatian sculptor Frano Kršinić, the statue shows Tesla in a sitting position reading blueprints. It is an identical copy of the monument standing in front of the Electrical Engineering building at the University of Belgrade in Serbia.

A second statue was dedicated in 2006. Sculpted by Les Drysdale, it shows a dignified Tesla standing elegantly atop one of his alternating current motors that made the harnessing of Niagara Falls for electricity possible. Befittingly, Tesla gazes out over the Horseshoe Falls on the Canadian side.

Keeping the Tesla Name Alive

Nikola Tesla has been largely forgotten by the history books and in the memories of today's public. Edison, Marconi, Röntgen, and others all roll off the tongue when we mention electricity, radio, X-rays. Yet Tesla contributed to all of these and did so in innovative ways.

Unlike the others, Tesla was not overly fond of commercialization of his discoveries and often worked secretly; in later life he became reclusive, poverty stricken, and more than a bit odd. These factors may help explain why he has been lost from memory.

But not completely lost. Google co-founder and CEO Larry Page has called Nikola Tesla his hero, although he did say it is better to be more like Edison than Tesla.[44] Page had read Tesla's autobiography *My Inventions* when he was twelve years old

Left: Tesla monument at Niagara Falls

and was fascinated by his amazing inventions. Tesla's problem, however, was that he did not know how to make money off of those inventions. In a 2008 interview with *Fortune* magazine, Page said:

"You also need some leadership skills. You don't want to be Tesla. He was one of the greatest inventors, but it's a sad, sad story. He couldn't commercialize anything, he could barely fund his own research. You'd want to be more like Edison. If you invent something, that doesn't necessarily help anybody. You've got to actually get it into the world; you've got to produce, make money doing it so you can fund it."[45]

Page says that Google is, in essence, a response to that failure. Innovate, but also sell it to the public so you can afford to innovate some more. With this in mind, Google has brought us a wide variety of inventions beyond its initial search engine—Android, the Chrome browser, Google Earth, Gmail—just to name a few. Not everything Google invented became a hit, of course, but enough did to keep the innovation rolling. That desire to combine the inventiveness of Tesla with the commercial marketing savvy of Edison has grown beyond Google into other investments. Both Larry Page and co-founder Sergey Brin have invested in something else that pays homage to Nikola Tesla—Tesla Motors. Exploiting several unique innovations in harnessing the power of electricity, the fully electric Tesla Roadster can go from zero to sixty miles per hour in under four seconds while also achieving 100 miles per gallon.[46] Now that is a high-performance sports car.

All you need is $100,000 to start (not counting options), or a friend named Larry Page.

Today there is a resurgence of interest in Nikola Tesla as a new generation of "science geeks" learn about his contributions and embrace his "weirdness." Several Tesla groups (not to mention the electric car company) have been working hard to keep the Tesla name alive.

The **Tesla Memorial Society of New York** (teslasociety.com) has been working since 2002 to have a United Nations-sanctioned "Nikola Tesla Day." A letter was sent on February 14th of that year to then-UN Secretary General Kofi Annan requesting a "Nikola Tesla Day—A World Day of Science." Progress was slow but in July 2012, Ban Ki-moon, the current General Secretary of the United Nations, was on a peace mission to the Balkan states of Serbia and Croatia. During his visit to Zagred he indicated that he supports the idea of a Tesla World Day of Science and recommended that an official request again be made to the U.N.

In Belgrade, the capital of present day Serbia, sits the **Nikola Tesla Museum**, which "holds more than 160,000 original documents, over 2,000 books and journals, over 1,200 historical technical exhibits, over 1,500 photographs and photo plates of original, technical objects, instruments and apparatus, and over 1,000 plans and drawings, all related to the life and work of Nikola Tesla." Tesla's "missing papers" are stored here, thanks to the efforts of Tesla's nephew, Sava Kosanovic,

Above: Tesla Mu\u0161eum in Belgrade, Serbia

who arranged their transfer in 1951, despite Tesla having become an American citizen. The archive was recognized by UNESCO for its critical role in safeguarding the history of the electrification of the world, although it appears that lack of funding has left many of Tesla's papers susceptible to water damage and lack of organization and security.[47]

The **Tesla Science Foundation** (http://teslasciencefoundation.org) was founded in Philadelphia with the goal of "promoting the legacy of Nikola Tesla by raising awareness of his accomplishments and contributions to the twenty-first century to include introducing his many patents and inventions that remain applicable to our current needs." The Foundation sponsors workshops, webinars, and meetings to communicate Tesla's contributions. They also select inventors who further the innovation inspired by Tesla and assist them through the patent process. Three awards per year are given "for achievements in technology, writing and art related to Tesla or his work."

The **Tesla Science Center at Wardenclyffe** (teslasciencecenter.org) was organized to develop a regional science and technology center on eastern Long Island. Rapidly growing out of its temporary space, the group hoped to establish a Tesla Science Center and Museum at Wardenclyffe, the last laboratory facility owned by Tesla. Abandoned in the early twentieth century, the site had several owners and, for nearly fifty years, was the site of the former Peerless Photo plant in Shoreham, New York. More recently it had been owned by Agfa, a division of Bayer Corporation, and over the past few years the Tesla Science Center negotiated with various stakeholders in hopes that the Tesla property could become the future home of the Tesla Science Center and Museum at Wardenclyffe.[48]

In August of 2012 a crowdfunding campaign was initiated in an effort to purchase the property against a rival bidder. Led by Matthew Inman, creator of an online cartoon site called *The Oatmeal* and unabashedly passionate about "the greatest geek who ever lived," the effort raised over $1 million in just nine days. This example of the awesome power of social networking was highly successful and the Tesla Science Center was able to purchase the property.

One thing is clear, however: many decades after his death, Nikola Tesla is alive and well in the hearts and minds of the populace. He would likely be very happy to see his final experimental laboratory site used to help educate and inspire the inventors of tomorrow.

Perhaps Thomas Commerford Martin best captured the essence of Tesla's genius, and his eccentricities, in his 1894 *The Century Magazine* article:

"Mr. Tesla has been held a visionary, deceived by the flash of casual shooting stars; but the growing conviction of his professional brethren is that because he saw farther, he saw first the low lights flickering on tangible new continents of science. The perceptive and imaginative qualities of the mind are not often equally marked in the same man of genius. Overplus of imagination may argue dimness of perception; an ability to dream dreams may imply a want of skill in improving reapers. Now and then the two elements combine in the creative poet of epic and drama; occasionally they give us the prolific inventor like Tesla."[49]

Above: Effect of electrical discharge from the earth illustrated by a Tesla coil

Let the future tell the truth,
and evaluate each one according to
his work and accomplishments.
The present is theirs;
the future,
for which I really worked,

is mine.

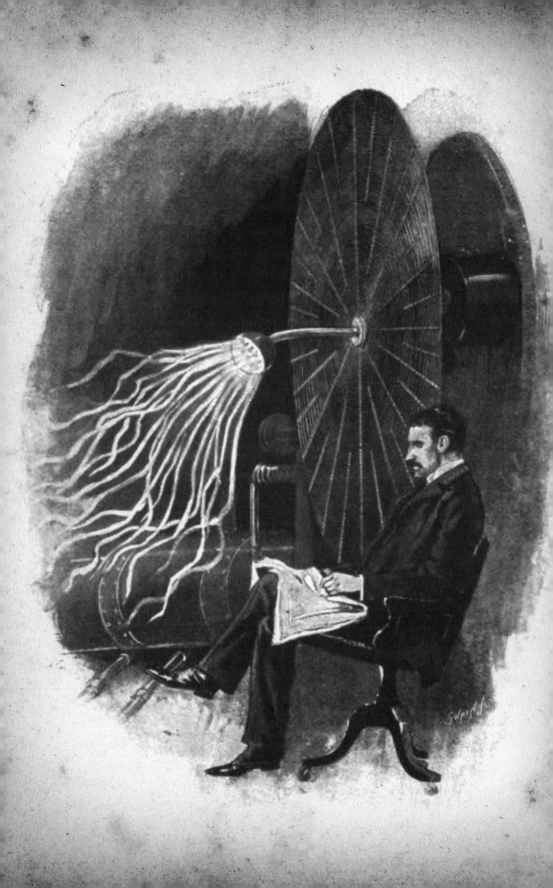

BIBLIOGRAPHY

- Aldrich, Lisa J. 2005. *Nikola Tesla and the Taming of Electricity*. Morgan Reynolds Publishing, Greensboro, NC.

- Barrett, John Patrick. 1894. *Electricity at the Columbian Exposition: Including an Account of the Exhibits in the Electricity Building a nd the Power Plant in Machinery Hall*. pp. 268-269. Accessible online at http://books.google.com/books?id=CLtIAAAAMAAJ&printsec =frontcover&hl=en#v=onepage&q&f=false.

- Carr, Nicholas. 2009. *The Big Switch: Rewiring the World, From Edison to Google*. W.W. Norton & Company, New York, NY.

- Cheney, Margaret. 1981. *Tesla: Man Out of Time*. Simon & Schuster, New York, NY.

- Cheney, Margaret and Uth, Robert, 1999. *Tesla, Master of Lightning*. Metro Books, New York, NY.

- *Collected Tesla Writings*. 2012. Scientific papers and articles by Nikola Tesla and others about Tesla's work primarily in the field of electrical engineering. Bottom of the Hill Publishing, Memphis, TN.

- Corum, Kenneth L. and Corum, James F. 1996. *Nikola Tesla and the electrical signals of planetary origin*. International Tesla Conference, "Tesla, III Millennium," Belgrade, Yugoslavia. 82 pp. Abstract accessible at http://www.tfcbooks.com/mall/planetary.htm.

- Dommermuth-Costa, Carol. 1994. *Nikola Tesla: A Spark of Genius*. Lerner Publications Company, Minneapolis, MN.

- Essig, Mark. 2003. *Edison & the Electric Chair: A Story of Light and Death*. Walker & Company, New York, NY.

- Jonnes, Jill. 2003. *Empires of Light: Edison, Tesla, Westinghouse, and the Race to Electrify the World*. Random House, New York, NY. Pages as in 2004 Random House Trade Paperback edition.

- Krause, Michael. 2011. *All About Tesla: How Nikola Tesla Invented the 20th Century*. Rich &Famous Publishing, Berlin, Germany. Position numbers as in Kindle version.

- Lomas, Robert. 1999. *The Man Who Invented the Twentieth Century*. Headline Book Publishing, London, UK.

- O'Neill, John J. 1944. *Prodigal Genius: Biography of Nikola Tesla*. Pages as in online version accessible at http://www.teslascience.net/library/text/Nikola-Tesla_biography/Prodigal-Genius,Biography-of-Nikola-Tesla.pdf.

- Martin, Thomas Commerford. 1894. *The Inventions, Researches and Writings of Nikola Tesla*. The Electrical Engineer, New York, NY.

- Martin, Thomas Commerford. 1894. "Nikola Tesla." *The Century Magazine*. February 1894. Accessible online at http://www.teslauniverse.com/nikola-tesla-article-nikola-tesla-2.

- Presentation of the Edison Medal to Nikola Tesla. Minutes of the Annual Meeting of the American Institute of Electrical Engineers, held at the Engineering Societies Building, New York City, Friday evening, May 18, 1917. Accessible online at http://www.tfcbooks.com/tesla/1917-05-08.htm.

BIBLIOGRAPHY

- Secor, H. Winfield. 1917. "Tesla's Views on Electricity and the War." *The Electrical Experimenter*. August 1917. Accessible online at http://www.tfcbooks.com/tesla/1917-08-00.htm.

- Seifer, Marc J. 1998. *Wizard: The Life and Times of Nikola Tesla: Biography of a Genius*. Citadel Press, New York, NY. Pages as in Citadel Press, First Printing, 1998 edition.

- Staley, Richard. 2009. "Albert Michelson, the Velocity of Light, and the Ether Drift." *Einstein's generation. The origins of the relativity revolution*. University of Chicago Press, Chicago, IL.

- Tesla, Nikola. 1888. "A new system of alternate current—motors and transformers." Lecture delivered before the American Institute of Electrical Engineers, May 16, 1888. Accessible online at http://www.tfcbooks.com/tesla/1888-05-16.htm.

- Tesla, Nikola. "Experiments with Alternate Currents of Very High Frequency and Their Application to Methods of Artificial Illumination." Delivered before the American Institute of Electrical Engineers, Columbia College, N.Y., May 20, 1891. Accessible online at http://www.tfcbooks.com/tesla/1891-05-20.htm.

- Tesla, Nikola. 1892. "Experiments with Alternate Currents of High Potential and High Frequency." A lecture delivered before the Institution of Electrical Engineers, London. Accessible online at http://www.tfcbooks.com/tesla/1892-02-03.htm.

- Tesla, Nikola. 1893. "On Light and Other High Frequency Phenomena." Delivered before the Franklin Institute, Philadelphia, February 1893, and before the National Electric Light Association, St. Louis, March 1893. Accessible online at http://www.tfcbooks.com/tesla/1893-02-24.htm.

- Tesla, Nikola. 1897. "On the Hurtful Actions of Lenard and Roentgen Tubes." *Electrical Review*. May 5, 1897.

- Tesla, Nikola. 1900. "The Problem of Increasing Human Energy." The *Century Illustrated Magazine*. June. Accessible online at http://www.tfcbooks.com/tesla/1900-06-00.htm.

- Tesla, Nikola. 1901. "Talking With Planets." *Collier's Weekly*. February 9, 1901. Accessible online at http://www.tfcbooks.com/tesla/1901-02-09.htm.

- Tesla, Nikola. 1904. "The Transmission of Electrical Energy Without Wires." *Electrical World and Engineer*. March 5, 1904. Accessible online at http://www.tfcbooks.com/tesla/1904-03-05.htm.

- Tesla, Nikola. 1915. "Some personal recollections." *Scientific American*, June 5, 1915. Accessible online at http://www.tfcbooks.com/tesla/1915-06-05.htm.

- Tesla, Nikola. 1919. "The True Wireless." *Electrical Experimenter*. May 1919. Accessible online at http://www.tfcbooks.com/tesla/1919-05-00.htm.

- Tesla, Nikola. 1927. "World System of Wireless Transmission of Energy." *Telegraph and Telegraph Age*, October 16, 1927. Accessible online at http://www.tfcbooks.com/tesla/1927-10-16.htm.

- Tesla, Nikola. 1931. "Our Future Motive Power," *Everyday Science and Mechanics*. December 1931. Accessible online at http://www.tfcbooks.com/tesla/1931-12-00.htm.

BIBLIOGRAPHY

- Tesla, Nikola as told to George Sylvester Viereck. 1937. "A machine to end war, A Famous Inventor, Picturing Life 100 Years from Now, Reveals an Astounding Scientific Venture Which He Believes Will Change the Course of History." *Liberty*, February 1937. Accessible online at http://www.tfcbooks.com/tesla/1935-02-00.htm.

- Wisehart, M.K. 1921. "Making Your Imagination Work for You." *American Magazine*. Vol. 91.

Other sources of information

- Twenty First Century Books series: http://www.tfcbooks.com/tesla/contents.htm
- Links to Patents by Nikola Tesla: http://www.teslascience.net/Nikola-Tesla_Patents.html
- Tesla Memorial Society of New York: http://www.teslasociety.com/
- Nikola Tesla Museum: http://www.tesla-museum.org/meni_en.htm
- Tesla Science Foundation: http://teslasciencefoundation.org
- Tesla Science Center at Wardenclyffe: http://www.teslasciencecenter.org/

Above: Lighting a single wire lamp through induction

223

1831 Faraday discovers electromagnetic interaction (precursor to alternating current)

1856 Born (stroke of midnight July 9–10) in Smiljan, a village near Gospić (a small town in Austrian Empire, now in the Republic of Croatia)

1861 Brother killed

1862 Family moves to Gospić

1866–1870 Attends "gymnasium" (junior high school); sees photo of Niagara Falls

1870 Moves from Gospić to Karlovac (Carlstadt) to attend a four-year high school; lives with father's sister Stanka and her husband; studies languages and mathematics and physics

1874 Contracts cholera and nearly dies; father concedes to allow him to study engineering instead of entering the clergy if he survives

1875 Enters the Polytechnical University at Graz for electrical engineering

1876 Witnesses Gramme dynamo at Graz; envisions a generator without a commutator

1876 Alexander Graham Bell invents telephone

1878 Leaves Graz without gaining a degree

1879 Employed as assistant engineer in Marburg for one year

1880 Attends University in Prague for summer term; father dies so Tesla leaves University

1881 Moves to Budapest and works for Puskas in a telegraph company; first invention is voice amplifier for the telephone receiver

1882 Has nervous breakdown; when recuperating quotes Faust and envisions alternating current motor in his head and draws the design in the dirt to show his friend Szigeti

1882 Moves to Paris to work for Continental Edison Company; advances induction motor and rotating magnetic fields ideas

1883–1884 Spends six months working on the reconstruction of faulty direct current generators in railroad power station in Strasbourg; makes the first model of the induction motor

1884 Returns to Paris. Feels cheated for not receiving promised payment for fixing the system in Strasbourg, but agrees to move to New York to work in the Edison Machine Works

1884 Arrives in U.S. with a letter of introduction from Charles Batchelor to Thomas Edison; meets Edison and fixes lighting plant aboard S.S. *Oregon*; Edison promises Tesla $50,000 to redesign direct current dynamos, then reneges a year later when work is complete

1885 Quits Edison feeling that he was cheated by him

1886 George Westinghouse forms Westinghouse Electric Company

1886 Forms Tesla Electric Light & Manufacturing Company; patent for electric arc lamp

1886–1887 Works as laborer; digs ditches; works on polyphase system design; gets first patent

1887 Forms Tesla Electric Company with Charles F. Peck and Alfred S. Brown; constructs initial alternating-current induction motor; begins investigating what would later be called X-rays

TESLA TIMELINE

1888 Invents the first practical alternating-current motor and polyphase power transmission system, which revolutionizes industry and commerce

1888 At urging of Thomas Commerford Martin, demonstrates to AIEE "A New System of Alternating Current Motors and Transformers"; receives five patents for his alternating motor; develops principles for Tesla coil; begins work with G. Westinghouse

1888 Westinghouse develops a meter that allows alternating current to be sold more efficiently

1888 Sells forty patents to Westinghouse for $60,000 including 150 shares of Westinghouse stock and $2.50 for each horsepower generated; moves to Pittsburgh; War of the Electric Currents begins

1889 William Kemmler is executed in an electric chair using alternating current

1890 Thomas Commerford Martin publishes full-page article on Tesla in *Electrical World*

1891 Early demonstration of wireless energy transmission; publishes paper in *Electrical World* in February and then gives lecture at AIEE event in May on high-frequency phenomena

1891 Invents Tesla coil

1891 Becomes a naturalized U.S. citizen on July 30

1891 Writes *The Inventions, Researches and Writings of Nikola Tesla,* edited by Thomas Commerford Martin

1892 Edison General Electric Company merges with Thomson-Houston Electric to create General Electric

1892 Gives lectures in London and Paris on his latest research ("Experiments with alternate currents of high potential and high frequency")

1892 While in Paris and London gets word of mother dying and goes back to Croatia, gets sick, but returns later to New York City

1893 Lectures in St. Louis on details of principles of radio (wireless) transmission; invents the first wireless transmission system

1893 Tesla systems used by Westinghouse to light the World Columbian Exposition in Chicago

1893 Guglielmo Marconi shows up in London with wireless equipment exactly as described by Tesla, denies ever hearing of Tesla's system

1893 Meets Robert Underwood Johnson and his wife, Katharine; demonstrates wireless lighting to dinner party guests

1894 Begins experimenting with high-frequency electromagnetic radiation; invents mechanical oscillators and generators of electrical oscillations

1895 Ready to transmit a radio signal a distance of fifty miles (80km), but then on March 13 his laboratory burns down; written up by Thomas Commerford Martin in *Engineering Magazine*

1895 Alternating current transmitted 500 miles (805km) for the first time at National Electrical Exposition in Philadelphia; Alexander Graham Bell quote re: "most important discovery of electric science"

1895–1896 Experiments with X-rays and shadowgraphs

1896 Electrical generation from Niagara Falls using his alternating-current system, November 16; rips up contract with Westinghouse, thus saving the company but losing many millions of dollars in royalties for life

1896 Marconi transmits radio waves through walls and over distances of several miles; Marconi patent denied because Tesla's already there, but Marconi moves forward

1897 Transmits radio signal from New York City to West Point

1898 Presents telautomaton (wireless controlled boat) at the Institute of Electrical Engineers Electrical Exposition in Madison Square Garden in May

1898 Moves into Waldorf-Astoria hotel

1899 Moves to Colorado Springs; develops "magnifying transmitter" (Tesla coil) to produce lightning and electrifies the ground for miles around; blows out the electric company's generator for Colorado Springs; receives communications he believes come from Mars from superior intelligence ETs

1900 Returns to New York City on January 8; starts work on wireless worldwide communication via Earth's ionosphere

1901 Construction on Wardenclyffe begins at Shoreham, Long Island, based on design by Stanford White and with funds from J. Pierpont Morgan

1901 Marconi transmits the letter "S" across the Atlantic using at least seven of Tesla's patents

1903 Tells J. Pierpont Morgan real reason for Wardenclyffe is to transmit wireless power, not just communication; Morgan withdraws support

1904 Marconi gets patent for the invention of radio (overturned in 1943)

1906 Invents bladeless turbine based on a new principle of the utilization of the energy of fluid by viscous friction

1907 Inducted into the New York Academy of Sciences in May

1907–1908 Develops designs for "flivver plane," which was eventually precursor to Marine Corps' V-22 Osprey vertical takeoff and landing plane; loses law-suit and Wardenclyffe equipment to Westinghouse

1909 Drafts plans for an aeromobile; makes first tests with steam and gas turbines

1909 Marconi receives Nobel Prize for "invention of radio"

1911–1913 Tests steam turbines in the Edison power plant in New York

1917 Works on a turbo-generator design

1917 Wardenclyffe demolished; awarded Edison Medal on May 18

1928 Applies for patents for the vertical takeoff and landing aeroplane

1931 On cover of *Time* magazine for seventy-fifth birthday; Edison dies

1936 Rumors of "death ray;" proposes projects to develop his telegeodynamics ideas and energy transmission through the Earth

1937 Robert Underwood Johnson dies (wife Katharine had died 1925)

1943 Dies on January 7 in New Yorker Hotel; government seizes estate

PHOTO CREDITS

DepositPhotos
© Oleg Kovalenko: 5; © Georgios Kollidas: 14, 30, 52, 74, 108, 130, 160, 176, 198

Courtesy Heritage Auction Galleries
2 bottom, 16 (lockets) bottom left & right, 49, 78, 187, 206

Courtesy Internet Archive
Patents of Nikola Tesla: 29 bottom, 51 bottom, 73 bottom, 107 bottom, 129 bottom, 159 bottom, 169, 175 bottom, 197 bottom; *Electrical Experimenter*: 146, 149, 156-157, 172, 188

Library of Congress
17 top, 19 (frame), 36-37, 42, 45, 59, 64, 65, 68, 72, 77, 79, 91, 93, 97, 98-99, 111, 120, 125, 127, 136-137, 155, 162, 174, 181, 185, 191, 210, 212

Private Collection
Endpapers, 3, 4 top, 6, 13, 16, 21, 56, 70, 86-87, 106, 133, 134, 139, 144-145, 171, 178, 194, 201, 219, 223, 239, 240; © *Real Heroes Comics*, 1946: 8, 47, 50, 71, 80, 83, 94, 104-105, 124, 126, 135,182, 189, 241; *Pearson's Magazine*: 27, 220, 224; *The Century Magazine*: 28, 66, 88, 116-117, 128, 138, 142, 154, 190, 218; *La Nature*: 40-41; *Galveston Daily News*: 60, 140; *Harper's Magazine*: 76; *Scientific American*: 85, 102, 166; *Chicago Tribune*: 119; *Radio Casopis*: 158; *Time Magazine*: 165; Courtesy *Popular Science*: 241, 243, 244, 245, 246, 247

Courtesy Scott Russo Archive
123

Science Source
© Sheila Terry: 114

Shutterstock
© brch photography: 17 bottom; © Hein Nouwens: 33; 82

Tesla Wardenclyffe Project
1, 2 top, 29 top, 51 top, 67, 73 top, 84, 100, 101, 107 top, 110, 122, 129 top, 148, 150, 152-153, 159 top, 175 top, 197 top, 203-204

Courtesy Wikimedia Foundation
16 (photos) bottom left & right, 19 photo, 42, 69, 213, 215, 216; *Scientific American*: 81; Michael Kleiman, US Air Force: 192

ENDNOTES

Prologue

1   O'Neill, *Prodigal Genius*, 138–140

Chapter 1: A Scientific Rock Star Is Born

1   O'Neill, 6
2   Dommermuth-Costa, *Nikola Tesla: A Spark of Genius*, 11-12
3   O'Neill, 8
4   Ibid.
5   Ibid.; Nikola Tesla Wikipedia (http://en.wikipedia.org/wiki/Nikola_Tesla). Languages were Serbo-Croat, German, Italian, French, English, Czech, Hungarian, Latin
6   O'Neill
7   Tesla, *My Inventions*
8   Tesla, Speech at acceptance of the Edison Medal, May 18, 1917
9   Tesla, *My Inventions*
10   Ibid.
11   Ibid.
12   Ibid.
13   Ibid.
14   Seifer, *Wizard: The Life and Times of Nikola Tesla: Biography of a Genius*, 66
15   Ibid.
16   Ibid.
17   Cheney, Uth, and Glenn, *Tesla, Master of Lightning*, 3
18   Tesla, *My Inventions*
19   Ibid.
20   Ibid.
21   O'Neill, 11
22   Ibid.; Tesla, *My Inventions*
23   O'Neill, 11
24   Tesla, Speech at acceptance of the Edison Medal, May 18, 1917
25   Tesla, *My Inventions*
26   Ibid.
27   O'Neill, 14
28   O'Neill, 17; Tesla, *My Inventions*
29   Ibid.
30   Ibid.
31   Tesla, "A Story of Youth Told by Age," http://www.pbs.org/tesla/ll/story_youth.html
32   Tesla, "Some Personal Recollections," *Scientific American*, June 5, 1915
33   Ibid.
34   Ibid.
35   Ibid.
36   O'Neill
37   Lomas, *The Man Who Invented the Twentieth Century*, 1999; Krause, *All About Tesla: How Nikola Tesla Invented the 20th Century*, 2011

ENDNOTES

Chapter 2: Coming of Age in Europe

1   http://en.wikipedia.org/wiki/Graz_University_of_Technology

2   http://www.presse.tugraz.at//pressemitteilungen/2006/16.05.2006_graz.htm
[via Google translate]

3   Seifer, 15

4   O'Neill, 33

5   Ibid.

6   Ibid.

7   http://www.presse.tugraz.at//pressemitteilungen/2006/16.05.2006_graz.htm
[via Google translate]

8   O'Neill, 33

9   Seifer, 15

10   Ibid.

11   Tesla, *My Inventions*

12   Ibid.

13   http://en.wikipedia.org/wiki/Gramme_machine

14   Tesla, *My Inventions*

15   http://en.wikipedia.org/wiki/Gramme_machine

16   http://en.wikipedia.org/wiki/Commutator_%28electric%29

17   O'Neill, 33

18   Ibid. 34

19   Krause, *All About Tesla: How Nikola Tesla Invented the 20th Century*, 685

20   Seifer, 17

21   O'Neill, 38

22   Seifer, 21

23   O'Neill, 38; Seifer, 21

24   Seifer, 20

25   Tesla, *My Inventions*

26   O'Neill, 39; Tesla, *My Inventions*

27   http://en.wikipedia.org/wiki/Budapest

28   Tesla, *My Inventions*

29   Ibid.

30   O'Neill, 42

31   Tesla, *My Inventions*

32   Ibid.

33   Cheney, *Tesla, Man Out of Time*, 54

34   Ibid., 101

35   Tesla, *My Inventions*; "Woodchoppers breakfast:" http://countrylife.lehmans.com/2011/
02/08/a-wood-choppers-breakfast/

36   Tesla, *My Inventions*

37   Seifer, 29

38   Tesla, *My Inventions*

39   Ibid.

40   Ibid.

41 Ibid.
42 O'Neill, 50; Tesla, *My Inventions*
43 Seifer, 30
44 O'Neill, 52

Chapter 3: The Odd Mr. Tesla

1 Tesla, *My Inventions*
2 Ibid.
3 Wisehart, "Making Your Imagination Work for You," *American Magazine*, 60
4 Tesla, *My Inventions*
5 Ibid.
6 Ibid.
7 Wisehart, 60
8 Tesla, *My Inventions*
9 Wisehart, 11
10 Tesla, *My Inventions*
11 Wisehart, 13
12 Tesla, *My Inventions*
13 Ibid.
14 Ibid.
15 Seifer, 16
16 Seifer, 207
17 Cheney, 139
18 Cheney, 279
19 Seifer, 413
20 Cheney, 141
21 Tesla, *My Inventions*
22 Ibid.
23 Cheney, 173
24 Krause, 1020
25 *New York Times*, November 12, 1907
26 Tesla, *My Inventions*
27 Cheney, 234
28 Cheney, 110
29 O'Neill, 265
30 Cheney, 110
31 Ibid.
32 O'Neill, 265
33 Ibid.
34 Ibid.
35 Jonnes, *Empires of Light: Edison, Tesla, Westinghouse, and the Race to Electrify the World*, 227
36 Seifer, 31
37 Tesla, *My Inventions*

38   Ibid.

39   Ibid.

40   http://www.ieee.org/about/awards/medals/edison.html

41   Ibid.

42   O'Neill, 205

43   Ibid.

44   Tesla, "On Light and Other High Frequency Phenomena," delivered before the Franklin Institute, Philadelphia, February 1893, and before the National Electric Light Association, St. Louis, March 1893. *The Inventions, Researches and Writings of Nikola Tesla*, 1893/4

45   Cheney, 307

Chapter 4: Of Edison and Westinghouse

1   Seifer, 31

2   Krause, 1115

3   Ibid.

4   Ibid.

5   http://en.wikipedia.org/wiki/Thomas_Edison

6   O'Neill, 53

7   Tesla, *My Inventions*

8   Ibid.

9   Ibid.

10   Seifer, 38

11   O'Neill, 55

12   Seifer, 39

13   Ibid. 31; Also, Arc lamp: http://en.wikipedia.org/wiki/Arc_lamp

14   Arc lamp: ibid.

15   Seifer, 41; Also Arc lamp ibid.

16   O'Neill; Tesla, *My Inventions*

17   Seifer, 41; O'Neill, 56

18   Ibid.

19   O'Neill

20   O'Neill

21   Seifer, 43

22   Tesla, *My Inventions*

23   Wisehart, 62

24   O'Neill, 58

25   Ibid.

26   Ibid.

27   Ibid., 59

28   Seifer, 43

29   Tesla, 1888 AIEE lecture: http://www.tfcbooks.com/tesla/1888-05-16.htm

30   O'Neill, 59; Note that "present time" was as of the date of publication in 1944

31   Seifer, 110

32 *Casablanca*: http://www.imdb.com/title/tt0034583/quotes

33 Jonnes, 310

34 O'Neill

35 Jonnes, 312

36 Seifer, 70

37 Jonnes, 312; Also, Martin, "Nikola Tesla" article in *The Century Magazine*, February 1894, 582

38 Lomas

39 O'Neill, 63

40 Ibid.

41 Seifer, 45

42 Krause, 1554

43 Ibid., 1558

44 Jonnes, 162

45 Ibid.

46 Ibid., 248

47 Ibid., 249

48 O'Neill, 89

49 Seifer, 100

50 Seifer, 117; Jonnes, 263

51 Seifer, 119

52 http://www.yeodoug.com/resources/dc_french/republic/dcfrench_republic. html; Note that the original statue was destroyed in a fire in 1896; a smaller twenty-four-foot bronze replica now stands in Jackson Park at the site of the Exposition's Electricity Building

53 Seifer, 119

54 Tesla, *My Inventions*

55 http://en.wikipedia.org/wiki/Niagara_Falls

56 Seifer, 134

57 O'Neill, 92

58 O'Neill, 105

Chapter 5: A Man Always at War

1 http://en.wikipedia.org/wiki/Thomas_Edison

2 Essig, 135

3 Carr, *Edison & the Electric Chair: A Story of Light and Death*, 38-39

4 Essig, 135

5 Ibid.

6 Ibid., 136

7 Ibid.

8 *New York Times*, October 12, 1889; Also from Dan Ariely, *The Upside of Irrationality*, 118-119, citing Zachary Shore's book *Blunder*

9 Essig, 92

10 Ibid., 93

11 Ibid., 99

12 Ibid., 140

13 Ibid, 142

14 Jonnes, 197, citing "For Shame, Brown!" *New York Sun*, August 25, 1889

15 Long, Tony. 2008. "Jan. 4, 1903: Edison Fries an Elephant to Prove His Point" http://www.wired.com/science/discoveries/news/2008/01/dayintech_0104

16 Carr, *The Big Switch: Rewiring the World, from Edison to Google*, 39

17 Essig, 255

18 Ibid., 252–253

19 Cheney, 230

20 O'Neill

21 Invention of Radio: http://en.wikipedia.org/wiki/Invention_of_radio

22 Ibid.; Tesla, *My Inventions*

23 Invention of Radio, Ibid.

24 Seifer suggests that Marconi might not actually have sent the letter "S" at that time.

25 Delmonico's: http://en.wikipedia.org/wiki/Delmonico%27s#Notable_patrons

26 O'Neill, 71

27 Tesla, *My Inventions*

Chapter 6: Wireless and Wardenclyffe

1   Wisehart, 64

2   Tesla, *My Inventions*

3   Wisehart, 64; Also, YouTube: http://www.youtube.com/watch?v=nQgO18qk1_k &feature=player_embedded

4   Wisehart, 64

5   O'Neill, 112

6   Barrett, *Electricity at the Columbian Exposition; Including an Account of the Exhibits in the Electricity Building, the Power Plant in Machinery Hall.* 268-269

7   Wisehart, 67

8   Ibid., 65

9   Tesla, *My Inventions*

10 Ibid., Also, Tesla, *Electrical Review*, November 1898

11 Tesla, *My Inventions*; also see "The Problem of Increasing Human Energy," *The Century Magazine*, June 1900

12 O'Neill, 143

13 Tesla, *My Inventions*

14 O'Neill, 154

15 Tesla, Colorado Springs Notebooks

16 O'Neill, 156

17 Tesla, "True Wireless," *Electrical Experimenter*, 1919

18 O'Neill, 157

19 Tesla, "The Transmission of Electrical Energy without Wires," *Electrical World and Engineer*, March 5, 1904

20 Ibid.

21 Tesla, *My Inventions*

22 http://en.wikipedia.org/wiki/Magnifying_transmitter

23 O'Neill, 162

24 Ibid., 163

25 Ibid., also, Tesla, Colorado Springs Notebooks

26 Tesla, *My Inventions*

27 Ibid.

28 O'Neill, 178

29 Tesla, *My Inventions*

30 http://en.wikipedia.org/wiki/World_Wireless_System#World_Wireless_System

31 Tesla, "World System of Wireless Transmission of Energy," *Telegraph and Telegraph Age*, October 16, 1927: http://www.tfcbooks.com/tesla/1927-10-16.htm

32 Tesla, *My Inventions*

33 *New York Times,* May 5, 2009: http://www.nytimes.com/2009/05/05/science/05tesla.html?_r=1&hp

34 http://en.wikipedia.org/wiki/Wardenclyffe_Tower#Theory_of_wireless_transmission

Chapter 7: Taking on Einstein

1 O'Neill, 215

2 Ibid.

3 Nobel Prize Organization, Nobel Prize Winners: http://www.nobelprize.org/nobel_prizes/physics/laureates/1921/; Note that Einstein actually received his 1921 prize in 1922 because the Nobel Committee for Physics had decided that none of the year's nominations met the criteria as outlined in the will of Alfred Nobel. According to the Nobel Foundation's statutes, the Nobel Prize can, in such a case, be reserved until the following year, and this statute was then applied. Albert Einstein therefore received his Nobel Prize for 1921 one year later, in 1922.

4 David Bodanis, $E = mc^2$: *A Biography of the World's Most Famous Equation*, New York: Walker, 2000; Also, http://en.wikipedia.org/wiki/Albert_Einstein

5 General theory of relativity: http://en.wikipedia.org/wiki/General_theory_of_relativity

6 *New York Times*, July 11, 1935

7 O'Neill, 216

8 Seifer, 102

9 *New York Herald Tribune*, September 11, 1932

10 Staley, Richard (2009), "Albert Michelson, the Velocity of Light, and the Ether Drift", *Einstein's generation. The origins of the relativity revolution*

11 Tesla, *My Inventions*

12 Tesla, "World System of Wireless Transmission of Energy," *Telegraph and Telegraph Age*, October 16, 1927

13 In 2011 the CERN laboratory near Geneva, Switzerland, claimed to have detected neutrinos traveling faster than the speed of light. A follow-up experiment confirmed the original results. However, other researchers have not been able to reproduce the

CERN results and they remain disputed at this time. http://en.wikipedia.org/wiki/Faster-than-light#Time_of_flight_of_neutrinos

14 *Time* http://www.teslasociety.com/time.jpg

15 Cheney, 294–295

16 *New York Herald,* Oct. 15, 1911

17 *New York Herald,* "Tesla's New Monarch of Machines," Oct 15, 1911

18 O'Neill, 31

19 Tesla patent 1,655,114; http://www.teslauniverse.com/nikola-tesla-patents-1,655,114–aerial-transportation

20 Seifer, 418

21 O'Neill, 134

22 Ibid.

23 Ibid.; Seifer

24 http://en.wikipedia.org/wiki/Thomas_Edison

25 Tesla, "On the Hurtful Actions of Lenard and Roentgen Tubes," *Electrical Review,* May 5, 1897

26 Tesla, "The Problem of Increasing Human Energy," *The Century Magazine,* June 1900

27 Secor, H. Winfield. "Tesla's views on electricity and the war," *The Electrical Experimenter,* August 1917

28 Ibid.

29 Cheney, 260

30 O'Neill, 134

Chapter 8: Beyond the Grave–Conspiracies Abound

1 "Tesla invents peace ray," *New York Sun,* July 10, 1934: http://www.tfcbooks.com/tesla/1934- 07-10.htm

2 Welshimer, Helen. *Every Week Magazine,* October 21, 1934: http://www.tfcbooks.com/tesla/1934-10-21.htm

3 O'Neill, 244

4 Ibid.

5 http://drvitelli.typepad.com/providentia/2009/08/the-tesla-conspiracy.html

6 Seifer, 446

7 Ibid., 447

8 Ibid., 456

9 http://drvitelli.typepad.com/providentia/2009/08/the-tesla-conspiracy.html

10 Ibid.

11 Tesla Museum, Belgrade: http://www.tesla-museum.org/meni_en.htm

12 "Nikola Tesla was murdered by Otto Skorzeny," posted by Vojislave Milosevic, February 13, 2012: http://www.veteranstoday.com/2012/02/13/nikola-tesla-was-murdered-by-otto-skorzeny/

13 http://swallowingthecamel.blogspot.com/2009/07/tesla-tales.html

14 "Is Tesla to Signal the Stars?," *Electrical World,* April 4, 1896

15   "Talking with Planets," *Colliers Weekly*, February 9, 1901: http://www.tfcbooks. com/tesla/1901-02-09.htm

16   Ibid.

17   Ibid.

18   Seifer, 468

19   http://en.wikipedia.org/wiki/Nikola_Tesla; Also, Corum, Kenneth L.; James F. Corum (1996). *Nikola Tesla and the electrical signals of planetary origin.* p.14

20   Seifer, 468; also, http://www.karmasurfer.com/genius.htm

21   http://en.wikipedia.org/wiki/John_Galt

22   http://www.only1egg-productions.org/AltSci/atlas_shrugged.htm

23   http://www.karmasurfer.com/genius.htm

24   http://listverse.com/2009/09/26/10-more-conspiracy-theories/

25   Tesla, *My Inventions*

26   http://www.youtube.com/watch?v=0K2wm8tn088

27   For example, see Seifer, 420

28   http://www.scienceforums.net/topic/21945-nikola-tesla/

29   http://www.haarp.alaska.edu/

30   http://listverse.com/2009/09/26/10-more-conspiracy-theories/

31   http://en.wikipedia.org/wiki/High_Frequency_Active_Auroral_Research_ Program

32   *New York Times*, "Edison and Tesla To Get Nobel Prizes," November 6, 1915

33   Cheney, 245; http://www.nobelprize.org/nobel_prizes/physics/laureates/

34   O'Neill, 201

35   *New York Times*, October 19, 1931

36   O'Neill, 130

Chapter 9: A Lasting Legacy

1   Tesla Museum, Belgrade: http://www.tesla-museum.org/meni_en.htm

2   O'Neill, 118

3   http://en.wikipedia.org/wiki/Nikola_Tesla; Tesla Memorial Society of NY http:// www.teslasociety.com/tesla_achievements.htm

4   Tesla, *My Inventions*

5   Seifer, 127

6   http://rationalwiki.org/wiki/Essay:Nikola_Tesla%27s_Wireless_Power Transmission

7   http://en.wikipedia.org/wiki/Tesla_coil

8   Krause, 1763

9   http://en.wikipedia.org/wiki/Tesla_coil#Applications

10   http://www.youtube.com/watch?v=216HO3idYJ8

11   http://en.wikipedia.org/wiki/Tesla_coil

12   http://en.wikipedia.org/wiki/Tesla_(band)

13   http://www.amazon.com/s/ref=sr_nr_i_7?rh=k%3Anikola+tesla%2Ci%3Apopu lar&keywords=nikola+tesla&ie=UTF8&qid=1340560289

14   www.teslaboy.com

15 http://www.amazon.com/Nikola-Tesla-At-Wardenclyffe-Tower/dp/B005K4JLBU/ref=sr_1_3?s=music&ie=UTF8&qid=1340560630&sr=1-3&keywords=nikola+tesla

16 http://www.youtube.com/watch?v=j5CfnJTR3Sg

17 http://www.amazon.com/s/ref=sr_nr_i_6?rh=k%3Anikola+tesla%2Ci%3Atoys-and-games&keywords=nikola+tesla&ie=UTF8&qid=1340560289

18 http://www.amazon.com/s/ref=sr_nr_i_5?rh=k%3Anikola+tesla%2Ci%3Aapparel&keywords=nikola+tesla&ie=UTF8&qid=1340560289

19 http://www.amazon.com/s/ref=sr_nr_i_8?rh=k%3Anikola+tesla%2Ci%3Asporting&keywords=nikola+tesla&ie=UTF8&qid=1340560289

20 Chair designed and built by Scott Mulcahey. Photograph by Charles Mulcahey

21 Seifer, 428

22 http://en.wikipedia.org/wiki/Frankenstein_%281931_film%29 citing Golman, Harry (November 11, 2005). *Kenneth Strickfaden, Dr. Frankenstein's Electrician.* McFarland & Company

23 http://www.imdb.com/title/tt0482571/

24 http://sanctuary.wikia.com/wiki/Nikola_Tesla

25 TED is an acronym for Technology, Entertainment, Design. Short (15–20 minute) talks by experts on a variety of topics are done in front of an audience and then made available online at http://www.ted.com/talks

26 *The Oatmeal*: http://theoatmeal.com/comics/tesla

27 http://www.ted.com/talks/lang/en/marco_tempest_the_electric_rise_and_fall_of_nikola_tesla.html. Also check out how they made the presentation: http://blog.ted.com/2012/06/20/marco-tempest-makes-the-early-1900s-new-again-as-he-tells-the-story-of-nikola-tesla/

28 Tesla, "A machine to end war, A Famous Inventor, Picturing Life 100 Years from Now, Reveals an Astounding Scientific Venture Which He Believes Will Change the Course of History," *Liberty,* February 1937, by Nikola Tesla as told to George Sylvester Viereck: http://www.tfcbooks.com/tesla/1935-02-00.htm

29 Nikola Tesla, Delivered before the American Institute of Electrical Engineers, Columbia College, N.Y., May 20, 1891. Experiments with Alternate Currents of Very High Frequency and Their Application to Methods of Artificial Illumination.

30 Tesla, "The Problem of Increasing Human Energy (with special references to the harnessing of the sun's energy)," *The Century Magazine,* June 1900

31 Ibid.

32 Tesla, *Philadelphia Public Ledger,* "Tesla 'Harnesses' Cosmic Energy," November 2, 1933

33 Tesla, "The Problem of Increasing Human Energy," *The Century Magazine*, June 1900

34 Ibid.

35 http://en.wikipedia.org/wiki/Robert_Underwood_Johnson

36 Siefer, 181

37 Ibid.

38 Tesla, "Our Future Motive Power," *Everyday Science and Mechanics*, December 1931

39 Tesla, "The Problem of Increasing Human Energy," *The Century Magazine*, June 1900

40   http://en.wikipedia.org/wiki/Tesla_(unit)

41   Aqua Survey, Inc., *R/V Tesla*: http://www.aquasurvey.com//services/r_v_tesla/

42   Personal communication, April 2, 2012

43   http://en.wikipedia.org/wiki/IEEE_Nikola_Tesla_Award

44   Serwer, Andy. 2008. "Larry Page on How to Change the World." *Fortune*, May 1, 2008. http://money.cnn.com/2008/04/29/magazines/fortune/larry_page_change_the_world.fortune/

45   Ibid.

46   http://www.teslamotors.com/roadster

47   http://en.wikipedia.org/wiki/Nikola_Tesla Museum; also, http://www.tesla-museum.org/meni_en.htm

48   http://www.teslasciencecenter.org/a-brief-history/

49   Martin, Thomas Commerford. 1894. "Nikola Tesla." *The Century Magazine*, February 1894

Above: Lighting a lamp through induction
Following: An undated picture of Tesla in his laboratory

ACKNOWLEDGMENTS

I wish to thank my agent, Marilyn Allen of Allen O'Shea Literary Agency, and my editor, Chris Barsanti at Sterling Publishing, for allowing me this opportunity to bring to life such a fascinating scientist and man as Nikola Tesla. The confidence they placed in me was as inspiring as Tesla's many contributions to society.

I also wish to thank the many family, friends, colleagues, and fellow scientists who have inspired and encouraged my scientific and writing careers over the years. They include Jamie Hobson, Alice Chen, Karin Ke, Rhys Daniels, Scott Krygier, Haiying Lin, Gulnur Bolyspayeva, Scott and Charlie Mulcahey, Nicole Darnall, my brother Don Kent, my son Bryan Kent, and many others. I want to give special thanks to Ru Sun for putting in many hours reading through multiple versions of the book. Her constant encouragement, constructive criticism, and amazing attention to detail have improved this book immeasurably.

I also thank all of the organizations that are working so hard to keep the Tesla name alive and make Wardenclyffe into a museum. Finally, I want to acknowledge all of the previous biographers who helped capture the life of Nikola Tesla. I hope that this present work has added some additional insights to the wonderful contributions each of you has offered.

Following: "Science Celebrates 100th Anniversary of Mr. Tesla, Who Made Work Easier," *Popular Science*, July 1956

TESLA DIED AT EIGHTY-SIX, ON JANUARY 7, 1943. IN SPITE OF THE HARDSHIPS THAT PLAGUED HIS LIFE, NIKOLA TESLA CONTINUED HIS SCIENTIFIC INVESTIGATIONS WHICH WERE SO FAR AHEAD OF HIS TIME.

Mr. Tesla, who made work easier

THE eyes of this man—Nikola Tesla (left)—saw the world of the covered wagon, into which he was born, turn into today's world of electricity, radio, and electronics, all within his lifetime. Other men also saw the change—and marveled at it. Tesla was not amazed: He planned it. He engineered it.

This month, engineering and scientific societies observe the 100th anniversary of the birth of this man who changed the world. Tesla was born about the time that sailing ships reached their peak—in the clippers. Before he was 40, he had invented the AC motor and long-distance transmission of electric power. By these two things alone, he made thousands of jobs easier everywhere—at home and at work. He also discovered many principles of radio and electronics. And even thought that he could broadcast power (as radio and TV are broadcast today).

Tesla about 40, at the height of his powers, is shown in the upper photo; in the lower portrait, he is near 80. Because of the vast change he made in the world, Tesla may be said, as much as anyone, to have "invented" Today. His life and work are shown on this and the next four pages.

1856 Nikola Tesla was born at midnight, July 9-10, in Smiljan, Croatia (now part of Yugoslavia). Little is known of his father. His mother could not read or write. But she could use her mind: She recited dozens of long poems and mechanically improved such household items as churns. Nikola showed flashes of scientific intuition from his early boyhood.

1857-60 In a world where 25 men scrounged a living with their muscles for every one who made a living any other way, Nikola, before he was five, played with another source of power. The use of wheels to harness water power was as old as history. From the disk of a tree trunk he made one, set it up as shown and watched as the current's force turned it.

1850s-60s In America, some men hauled carts by hand from the Missouri River to Salt Lake. Horses worked just as hard: The Pony Express raced mail from St. Joseph, Mo., to San Francisco in 10 days. In Croatia, Nikola, seven, saw a fire engine that wouldn't pump water. Intuitively, he diagnosed the trouble. He dived into the river and unkinked the hose.

1865 The world struggled with a new power —inefficient, dirty, hissing steam. In four years men would complete (by hand) a track across the U. S. Tesla, nine, struggled with another power: He made a tiny windmill, glued four June bugs to the blades. Their beating wings turned the blades, and a spindle. He dreamed of a 100-bugpower machine but never built it.

1884 "No more will men be slaves to hard tasks," Tesla said. "My motor will set them free." But no one would give him financial backing. He sailed to the U.S., lost his baggage, his model—all but four cents. But of all the 518,592 immigrants who arrived in '84, he would change the country most. His mind carried all the plans for making it possible.

1885-87 Tesla met and worked for Edison. But Edison was no readier for AC than Europe had been. The arguments were vigorous. Tesla and Edison described each other's mentality as low. Tesla quit his job with the inventor. Soon he was reduced to the drudgery that the world was full of. He became a day laborer and went to work as a ditchdigger.

1866-80 Steam power spread. An engine reached Croatia. Nikola, about 14, saw it—the first man-made source of power he had ever seen. He also saw a snowball, rolling downhill, become an avalanche. He noted that accumulated ounces of snow had turned into a great, moving power. He saw a picture of Niagara Falls, and said, "Some day I'll harness that."

1882-83 After Thomas Edison opened his first plant—DC—to light lamps of his 59 nearby customers, the world grew dimly aware of the wonders of electricity. In Europe, Tesla, 25, thought that electricity could also provide power. Needed: an AC motor, thought to be as impossible as perpetual motion. He dreamed up the plans and made a model. It ran.

1888 Suddenly Tesla hit the jackpot. He got patents on his AC motor and impressed the American Institute of Electrical Engineers (this month celebrating his 100th birthday) with a lecture which explained his idea. George Westinghouse, a competitor of the famous Edison, gave Tesla, the recent ditchdigger, a million dollars for the patent rights to his motor.

1889-90 Working together, Westinghouse and Tesla soon evolved AC motors and dynamos of many sizes. Tesla built a high-voltage coil—the Tesla coil—that with one end inert, the other spouting thousands of volts, would light lamps placed on the other side of the room—without using wires. This was the beginning of his attempts to broadcast power.

1892 To concentrate on work, Tesla ruled out romance. If his discoveries looked impossible in those days of warring Indians, skinny-tired bicycles, and horsecar commuting, he did something—for a man—which was considered more impossible. The "divine" actress, Sarah Bernhardt, dropped her handkerchief before him. He returned it—without saying a word.

1893 The big shows were the late P. T. Barnum's, Buffalo Bill's, Sarah Bernhardt's and —at the World's Columbian Exposition—Little Egypt dancing the hoochee-coochee. Westinghouse and Tesla lighted and powered the Exposition, an accomplishment that finally sold the doubting U. S. on AC. Tesla himself lighted glass tubes without using any wires.

1899-1900 Tesla thought that the earth was electrically charged. (It is.) At Colorado Springs, he set up a plant that would add to the earth's charge so you could plug in anywhere and get electricity. He pumped power in, claimed to draw it back—creating lightning. Unfortunately, he never wrote down the details of his experiments for future reference.

1901-16 At a time when radio consisted only of dot-dash messages, Tesla set out to build, on Long Island, N. Y., a radio city that would broadcast both power and all the kinds of programs that are known to such widespread audiences today. Tesla never got around to broadcasting either. But he did discover many fundamentals of radio. Then he went broke.

1895-96 Westinghouse and Tesla put on their biggest show. They built a powerhouse at Niagara Falls. General Electric, with Tesla methods, built a 22-mile transmission line to Buffalo. This was a significant advance. Edison had delivered power about a mile. Here power went from one area to another. The age of sending power far and wide had dawned.

1898 The U. S.'s Admiral George Dewey licked the Spaniards in Manila Bay. Tesla, at Madison Square Garden, put a boat equipped with radio in a tank of water. From afar, he started, steered, and lighted the vessel—by radio. It was, he said, the first of a race of robots that would fight—operated by remote control—in the future wars of the world.

1920s-30s Growing old, Tesla withdrew even more into himself. This man, who was responsible for every AC motor (162 million horsepower when he died), and every transmission tower and line, kept his blinds closed—except during storms. Then he would throw open his windows, lie down on a couch and watch the lightning dance across the sky.

1930s-40s The world last saw Tesla on the steps of the New York Public Library. He had found a love: Daily he fed the pigeons. The man who had made work easier for millions all over the world was the old man whom unknowing thousands saw feeding the pigeons. On January 7, 1943, at 86, Nikola Tesla died alone in a New York hotel room. **END**

David J. Kent has 30 years of scientific research, consulting, and writing experience. He has given over 100 presentations at regional, national, and international scientific meetings, as well as taught short courses on a variety of scientific topics. He specializes in communicating science in ways that the general public can understand. Through inspiring life stories, clear common language explanation of sometimes confusing scientific subjects, and reviews of relevant books, David J. Kent makes science fun again.

He has been President of the Regional Chapters of both the Society of Environmental Toxicology and Chemistry and the Society for Risk Analysis. His writing includes numerous publications in peer-reviewed scientific journals, technical newsletters, and general interest publications. An avid traveler—having lived overseas several times in his life—and an Abraham Lincoln aficionado, he has written numerous articles on both topics. In communicating science to the general public, sometimes the science is historical, as in biographies of Nikola Tesla and Abraham Lincoln. Sometimes the science is instructional, as in distilling the dry, technical language of climate change into something everyone can relate to their lives. And sometimes his writing is just a fun way to express a love of travel, such as asking whether Galileo really did drop balls from the Leaning Tower of Pisa, and if he did, was anyone there to catch them?

You can find David J. Kent at *Science Traveler* (www.davidjkent-writer. com), on Twitter (@davidjkentwrite), and on LinkedIn.